Six Feet
The Only Resting Place

A Journey through Life, Death, and the Spaces in Between

by

Anosike Igwe

Copyright © 2025 by
Anosike Igwe

ALL RIGHTS RESERVED. No part of this book may be reproduced or transmitted in any form by any means, electronic or mechanical, including photocopying and recording, or by any information storage and retrieval system, except as may be expressly permitted in writing from the author.

ISBN: Paperback: 978-1-969066-92-4

Hardcover: 978-1-969066-93-1

Published by

Dany Book Publishers LLC

www.danybookpublishersllc.com

Printed in the United States of America

Dedication

To God Almighty, the source of my strength, my vision, and every gift within me. Without Your grace, this book would not exist.

To my mother, **Janet Igwe**, whose unwavering love, sacrifice, and prayers shaped the foundation of who I am. I owe my beginnings and my becoming to you.

To my first mentor after my mother, **Moses Enenwali**, thank you for guiding my steps, sharpening my purpose, and believing in my potential long before the world could see it.

To my beloved wife, **Sandra Igwe**, and our daughters, **Miracle Ezinne Igwe** and **Emmanuella Chinenyenwa Igwe**, you are my heart, my inspiration, and my daily reminder of why I must keep striving. Your love fuels every page of this work.

Anosike Igwe

Acknowledgment

I give all glory, honor, praise and adoration to God Almighty, whose grace, wisdom, and strength made this work possible. Every page of this book is a testimony to His faithfulness in my life.

To my father and mother, Mr. Igwe Nwachukwu and Mrs. Janet Igwe; my cousin, Grace Igwe-Okezie; my childhood friend, Liman Attahiru; Prince Emmanuel Ikpeagha; and my spiritual mother, Pastor Sarah Omakwu: your sacrifices, prayers, and steadfast belief in my potential have carried me farther than words can express. You planted within me the courage to dream and the discipline to achieve.

To my first mentor after my mother, Architect Moses Enenwali, thank you for guiding me, challenging me, and investing in my growth. Your influence helped shape the voice and vision behind this work.

To my wife, Sandra Igwe, your unwavering support, patience, and love have been my anchor throughout this journey. You stood with me through every late night, every revision, and every moment of doubt. I am forever grateful.

To my daughters, Miracle Ezinne Igwe and Emmanuella Chinenyenwa Igwe, you are my inspiration. Your joy, curiosity, and brilliance remind me of the importance of leaving a legacy worth inheriting. This book is as much yours as it is mine.

I also extend my heartfelt appreciation to every friend, teacher, supporter and Dany Book Publishers LLC who offered encouragement, feedback, or simply believed in this mission. Your kindness has fueled my determination.

Finally, to every reader who picks up this book, thank you. Your time and openness breathe life into these words.

About the Author

Anosike Igwe was born to humble parents from Eastern Nigeria (Abia State) and raised in the middle belt (Nasarawa State), where hardship shaped both his character and imagination. The seventh of nine children and the first surviving child, he knew early the weight of struggle and the quiet strength of resilience. When poverty threatened to end his education, a divine encounter with Architect Moses Enenwali opened a door that changed the course of his life. His mother, Janet Igwe, sacrificing even the clothes on her back, became the living embodiment of courage and devotion that continues to inspire his work.

From those beginnings, Anosike pursued knowledge with relentless determination, eventually earning bachelor's degrees in Technical Management and a master's degree in Cybersecurity in the United States of America, and serving honorably in the United States Navy for over eighteen years now. Through every chapter of his journey, he carried with him an unwavering belief that the future holds light for those who believe that once there is life, there is hope.

A writer of fiction whose stories echo truth, endurance, and the human spirit, Anosike weaves narratives shaped by faith, memory, and the landscapes of his childhood. His work blends poetic introspection with the grit of lived experience, offering readers windows into resilience, transformation, and the quiet triumphs of the soul.

He is inspired daily by his wife, Sandra, and their daughters, Miracle and Emmanuella, whose love remains the heartbeat of his creativity.

This book stands as another piece of evidence of his enduring mission: to tell stories that matter, stories that heal, uplift, and illuminate the hidden greatness within us all. Additionally, as a fiction writer, he draws deeply from memory, faith, and the human condition. His stories also echo courage, loss, resilience, and the beauty of rising again.

Note to the Reader

Hello Amazing Reader!

Welcome to this thrilling adventure of words and worlds! This book was born from a whirlwind of inspiration, late-night brainstorming sessions, and a caffeine-fueled passion that just wouldn't quit. It all started as a casual conversation among friends, where ideas bounced around like popcorn in a hot pan, igniting the spark that led to this moment. Can you feel the excitement? I hope so! Grab your favorite drink and get comfy because we're diving into something extraordinary.

The research that went into this book was nothing short of a rollercoaster ride. I explored ancient texts, modern interpretations, interviewed experts on subjects that blew my mind, and even embraced some unconventional sources. Every chapter you see here is infused with hard-hitting facts, creative notions, and the kind of passion that gets your heart racing. This isn't just a book; it's a labor of love that reflects hours of dedication.

Why did I write this book? Well, I wanted to spark curiosity, challenge perspectives, and perhaps even shake things up a bit. There's so much static in the world of literature today, and I wanted this piece to be a fresh breeze through an open window, inviting you to join me on a journey that pushes boundaries and defies norms. I believe stories can heal, educate, and inspire, and that's exactly what I hope to deliver within these pages.

Now, let's talk about what you can expect. Each section has been crafted not just to inform you but to engage and provoke thought. Expect laughter, perhaps a few tears, and definitely a whole lot of revelations. You might be surprised by how much you learn about yourself through the characters and scenarios woven into this narrative. I've poured my heart and soul into every word, and I can't wait to share it all with you.

As you read on, I encourage you to pause, reflect, and interact with the content. Mark your favorite passages, doodle in the margins, or even jot down your own thoughts. This book isn't just a one-way conversation; I want to hear from you! Let's connect over the themes and ideas that resonate.

Even if the journey gets a bit bumpy, hang in there, growth often comes with a side of discomfort! Reaching the end of this book won't just leave you with conclusions; I hope you walk away with questions that inspire further exploration. You might find yourselves pondering the themes long after you finish the last page. That's the magic I'm aiming for!

So, are you ready to turn the page and jump in? Trust me, it'll be worth your while. Each chapter is a steppingstone toward greater understanding, a ticket to a wild ride through imagination and insight.

And remember, every great adventure starts with a single word. Thank you for allowing me to take you on this exhilarating journey. Let's see where the path leads you!

With every twist and turn, I invite you to explore the unknown. There's something beautiful about venturing into uncharted territory, and that's where the real treasure lies. Your thoughts and interpretations will bring this experience to life, making it uniquely yours. So don't hesitate, dive into this sea of ideas and let the waves carry you!

I can't wait to hear what you think and how this book resonates with you. Your adventure awaits, and the pages are ready to be explored. Let's embark on this journey together, hand in hand, thought by thought, word by word.

With excitement and anticipation, I present to you the pages that follow. Buckle up and enjoy the ride!

With all the enthusiasm in my heart,
Anosike Igwe

Table of Contents

Whispers from the Grave 1

    The Forgotten Stories 2

    Echoes of Regret 9

    Lessons from the Beyond 16

The Color of Memories 27

    A Palette of Emotions 28

    Blending the Past and Present 36

    The Vibrancy of Love 42

Ember of Traditions 48

    Rituals of Remembrance 49

    The Comfort of Shared Stories 56

    Transforming Grief into Celebration 65

A Garden of Fragile Wishes 72

    Finding Sanctuary in Nature 73

    Planting Seeds of Remembrance 79

    The Blooms of Resilience 86

The Void of Unlived Life 96

    Confronting the Unfulfilled 97

  Embracing the Courage to Live 104

  Honoring What Could Have Been 116

Serenade of the Stars 125

  A Night of Reflection 126

  Whispers of the Cosmos 133

  The Dance of Life 141

Closure in the Chaos 148

  Embracing Life's Unpredictability 149

  Finding Solace in Disarray 156

  Lessons from the Storm 166

The Language of Silence 173

  Navigating Quiet Spaces 174

  The Unsaid Bonds 180

  Communicating Through Presence 188

Existential Threads 196

  Tapestries of Connection 197

  Unity Amidst Diversity 204

  The Strength of Shared Stories 212

Whispers from the Grave

The Forgotten Stories

The air was thick with nostalgia, the kind that settled in the lungs and prompted a deep, reflective sigh. The protagonist stood at the entrance of a forgotten cemetery, its iron gates rusted and heavy with the weight of time. Wild overgrowth sprawled across the path, as nature slowly reclaimed what had once been meticulously manicured lawns and orderly rows of vibrant flowers. For many, this sacred ground was little more than a memory, an obscured chapter in the larger narrative of life. For the protagonist, it was a portal, a threshold beckoning them into a world filled with whispers, secrets, and stories long left unspoken.

As they stepped inside, the crunch of gravel beneath their feet punctuated the silence, drawing the attention of ghostly murmurs swirling through the air. It was almost imperceptible at first, a faint current of sound woven through the rustling leaves. The protagonist paused, heart thrumming as they listened more intently, discerning the whispers just beyond the veil of stillness. Each voice seemed to carry with it fragments of lived experience, echoes of lives that once danced vibrantly in the light. The weathered tombstones stood like sentinels, each one a keeper of secrets, silent yet insistent in their call to be remembered. The protagonist drifted through the rows, fingers grazing the cool surfaces of the stones, tracing the engraved names and dates that marked the passage of time. They felt a peculiar intimacy with these markers of mortality; each one encapsulated a unique existence; a narrative of joy and sorrow entwined in the rich tapestry of human experience.

"Will you listen?" the wind seemed to whisper, threading through the branches above, encouraging them to delve deeper into the histories laid to rest beneath the earth.

The protagonist closed their eyes, allowing the sound to envelop them, a shroud of tales waiting to be absorbed. Memories began to flood their mind, intermingling with the hushed voices that surrounded them. With each step, they felt drawn toward a particular grave at the end of a weathered path, one that stood proudly amid the encroaching chaos of weeds and ivy. The headstone was aged and cracked, the inscription barely legible but still potent in its simplicity:

"Here lies William Calder, 1823 – 1895."

An inexplicable gravitational pull urged the protagonist forward, inviting them to kneel beside the grave. As they settled on the cool, damp ground, a shimmering light began to materialize before them. The air crackled with energy, and from the shimmer emerged the spirit of a long-gone ancestor. He appeared like a gentle silhouette, an ethereal figure clothed in soft, flowing robes that danced with the wind, revealing the timeless essence of who he had once been.

"Hello, child of my blood." His voice resonated like distant thunder, powerful yet soothing. "I have waited long to share my stories with one of our lineages."

The protagonist felt a shiver of recognition, a bond that transcended the bounds of time and space. With a nod, they indicated their willingness to listen, and the spirit's expression softened, an effect as warming and captivating as sunlight breaking through ominous clouds.

"Each soul that inhabits this ground has something to teach us," he began. "Whispers carried by the winds are not just echoes; they are lifelines back to the moments that shaped us."

William's voice wove a tale of love and longing, recounting the heights of happiness and depths of despair he had experienced. He spoke of his youth spent in the embrace of nature, where it was said that even the trees whispered secrets to him. Memories flowed effortlessly, revealing a life of commitment to family, struggle, and a fierce desire to leave a lasting legacy.

"There was a time when my beloved Margaret and I dreamt of growing old together, sharing laughter under the starlit sky," he said, a sense of reverence surrounding the name of his lost love. "Yet fate intervened, and in the blink of an eye, our connection was severed. I learned to navigate the shadows of grief, to carry her memory as a lantern before me, a guiding light through the darkest nights."

With each story, the protagonist felt the aching weight of love and loss, a palpable connection that reached deep into the marrow of their being. William's accounts became a bridge, spanning generations and beckoning them to reflect on their own familial narratives. The emotion laced with their ancestor's words evoked vivid visions: gatherings by the fire, shared meals steeped in tradition, laughter punctuated by tears. These memories weren't merely remnants of the past; they were threads binding the present with the weight of legacy.

"Every grave represents a unique story," William continued, gesturing toward the surrounding tombstones that swayed gently in the breeze. "Do you see them? Each one, known and cherished in ways that often go unspoken, and buried beneath the soil like seeds waiting to bloom."

The protagonist gazed at the headstones, each bearing witness to a life once full of dreams and aspirations. They felt an overwhelming urge to uncover those stories, fragments of history woven into the very earth beneath their fingers. It was a reminder that while grief might silence the living, the dead have a way of weaving their narratives into the hearts of those who remain.

"Learn from their tales," William urged gently. "The whispers you hear are not merely echoes of loss, but a symphony of resilience. Understand that every sorrow carried is a testament to love."

As he spoke, other spirits began to appear around the grave, their forms shimmering in the soft light. Each seemed to glow with tales of their own stories etched into the very essence of their beings. The protagonist looked around in awe, eyes wide with the revelation of the collective histories converging at this single point, the intersection of existence and memory. A woman dressed in a flowing gown of lavender appeared beside William, her hair cascading like tendrils of light.

"I was Edith," she spoke with a melodic tone. "I lost my husband in the war, and grief threatened to consume my spirit. But I found solace in my children; I wove their childhoods around the fabric of my lost dreams. They became my purpose; a reminder that love endures even when loss seems insurmountable."

The protagonist felt a tear escape as they listened to the weight of her recounting the delicacy of motherhood tethered to the deep ache of absence. It was an acknowledgment of the intricacies of life woven through joy and sorrow alike. As Edith shared her heartache, the protagonist sensed a profound truth: love is inherent in our stories, and the strength of connections shapes us in unimaginable ways. Each voice that followed resonated with similar themes of resilience. Some shared tales of longing, others of triumph against adversity. The recounting formed a symphony of shared experiences that transcended time, an assurance that while life had its endings, it also spun new beginnings.

A gentle mist began to envelop the area, capturing the protagonist's attention. It felt ethereal and surreal, inviting them deeper into this sacred space.

"You see, the stories are waiting to be uncovered," William concluded, a softness in his gaze that pierced through the barriers of time. "But it is up to you to listen, to heed their lessons, and to carry them forth as part of your own narrative."

As each spirit drifted away, leaving behind an echo of their essence, the protagonist sat in silence, contemplating how these forgotten stories nestled within the tombstones resonated with their own life. They felt the connection to their roots, the web of family history that intertwined through generations. Through love and loss, pain and joy, each person remembered vividly, with memories capable of igniting hope among the living. The sun began to dip below the horizon, casting a warm golden glow over the cemetery. The protagonist's heart swelled with gratitude for the stories shared, for the whispers of their ancestors that would forever dwell within. It was an understanding that every soul laid to rest carried dreams and aspirations, irrevocably woven into the fabric of existence.

More importantly, they understood that their ancestors' tales weren't just relics of the past but gifts that held the power to illuminate the present and guide their future. With a newfound sense of purpose, the protagonist rose from beside William's grave. The wind murmured through the trees, as if urging them to step forth with the knowledge that love never dies; it transforms, igniting the flames of remembrance and resilience. Even amidst the sorrow, there is beauty to be found in the stories that linger, whispering across time in a powerful plea to honor shared histories.

As they exited the cemetery, a reviving sensation coursed through their being. Each step was lighter than the last, propelled by the promise of uncovering the stories yet to be told. They embarked on a journey, one that beckoned exploration of familial narratives rich with emotion, complexity, and the profound significance of shared memory. And though the graves would remain silent guardians to the lives once lived, the whispers of their stories would resonate through the ages, carried on the winds of time and forever woven into the heart of existence.

Echoes of Regret

The moon hung low in the sky, casting a silver glow over the cemetery, turning tombstones into jagged silhouettes against the night. As the protagonist stepped cautiously along the cobblestone path, a chill swept through the air, a whisper of what was to come. The ethereal environment hummed with stories untold, yet one voice seemed to rise above the rest, calling out from the depths of sorrow and longing. It was then that the air around the protagonist thickened, and where there had just been night, a shimmering figure swirled into view. The ghostly presence stood before the protagonist, an outline of translucent light, woven from the threads of memory and regret. The spirit's eyes, pools of unfiltered emotion, spoke of lives unfinished, of possibilities that evaporated like morning mist.

The ghost appeared bewildered yet resolute, an embodiment of longing that reverberated through the stillness like a mournful song. The protagonist's heart raced, caught between fear and an insatiable curiosity. They had come to this place with questions of their own, seeking the comfort of connection amidst loss. Yet, here was a spirit begging for recognition, a soul tied to their experience through threads of time and emotion. As the air crackled with tension, the protagonist sensed their own fears murmuring within, a reminder of the unresolved stories in their own life. I wish I could turn back time, the ghost spoke, their voice a fragile whisper caught in the wind. There were so many things left unsaid, so many moments that slipped through my fingers as though they were grains of sand. The spirit's words hung heavily in the air, echoing with the weight of unspoken desires and neglected aspirations.

"What do you regret the most?" the protagonist dared to ask, feeling an unfamiliar tug at their heartstrings, an invitation to delve deeper.

The ghost inhaled sharply, as if gathering courage before unveiling the intimate tapestry of their lifetime, a patchwork steeped in vibrant colors of unfulfilled dreams.

"Love. It was the love I didn't express that haunts me." The ghost's voice trembled, laden with sorrow. "I had someone waiting for me, yet I let fear dictate my choices. I kept my heart locked away, afraid of vulnerability. And in that silence, I lost them."

The protagonist felt an overwhelming swell of empathy, their own past casting shadows over their present as they listened to the spirit unravel their story. The protagonist was immediately transported to moments in their own life, echoes of silenced pleas and dreams stifled by self-doubt. Memories flooded back, unresolved confrontations with honesty that they, too, had failed to embrace.

"I wish I had been brave enough to say the words that danced so close to my lips," the ghost continued. "Each unspoken confession turned into a chain, binding me to the regrets of my existence. And now, here I am, a remnant of the life I never fully lived."

In the dim light of the moonlit cemetery, the protagonist placed their hand upon the cold stone of a nearby grave, drawing strength from the connection between the living and the lost.

"Was it worth it, then? All this regret?" The question floated into the air, full of both challenge and curiosity. Silence enveloped them, a moment of shared understanding where the weight of unfulfilled aspirations loomed large.

"Perhaps the worth lies in the lessons learned," the ghost mused, their form flickering slightly, a balance between the past and the present. "But would I give anything to take away the sting of my choices and the silence that enveloped my heart? Yes, a thousand times over."

With each word, the ghost's essence shimmered more brightly, and the protagonist understood that regret flowed from a longing to connect, to love, to live without the constraints of fear. What struck the protagonist the most was this haunting sense of mirrored reflections. They, too, had held their truth prisoner; fears of judgment and uncertainty had muffled their voice. They had constructed barriers, unaware of how those barriers could also enclose the joy and authenticity that life offered. Listening to the spirit, an inescapable truth emerged that every moment spent in silence was a moment stolen from potential happiness.

The ghost's ethereal presence deepened, shimmering with unspoken truths, and the protagonist, inspired by a strange kinship, pressed further. "What kept you from being honest? Why didn't you confront your fears?"

The query bore weight, each syllable inviting vulnerability from both sides as they gravitated towards truth.

"It was the peril of vulnerability," the ghost sighed, each word heavy with gravity. "I feared the rejection, the heartbreak, and the potential for loss itself. Each time I considered risk, I opted for the convenience of acquiescence instead. But now, standing here without the warmth of my love, I long for that connection so desperately that it renders me restless. I should have embraced the chaos of living, but I chose a quieter path, one filled with emptiness instead."

As the air pulsed with the intensity of regret, the protagonist felt their own heart quicken. Flashes of their life played out like a reel, encapsulating moments of miscommunication, silenced confessions, and paths never taken. They understood the ghost's anguish and recognized it intertwined with their own, pulling them into the depths of shared remorse.

"How can I find your courage?" the protagonist asked quietly, almost as if the simple act of uttering the question held the key to their own self-discovery. "I want to break free from my own regrets and live more authentically."

The ghost seemed to pull closer, their essence radiating warmth. "Courage isn't found; it is built through confrontation. You must face the fears that weigh you down. Speak your truths, even when your voice shakes. It is through disclosing pain and vulnerability that you create connections, and those connections can transcend even death."

The passion in the spirit's voice reverberated against the hallowed ground, each word a step toward liberation. In that moment, something deep within the protagonist stirred. Faces came alive with vibrant energy, people who had been abandoned by unspoken words, who had waited for the very conversations lost in time. The timeliness of this meeting became a conduit for connecting lives and memories, both past and present, exemplifying the timeless struggle against regret.

"It's never too late for honesty," the ghost continued, imbued with urgency. "Even for me. My body may be gone, but my voice still echoes through your choices. And with every moment you choose to live authentically, my existence gains meaning. The weight of regret diminishes when love persists."

The protagonist's heart raced as the understanding crystallized that the journey of self-discovery was not only about erasing regret but rather embracing love, connection, and raw, unfiltered truth. The regret that burdened the ghost had become a teacher, imparting wisdom and encouragement rather than lingering solely as a shadow.

"Thank you," the protagonist whispered, their voice trembling with realization. "Your words will shape my path from now on. I will carry your story and transform it into action, allowing the echoes of your life to resonate within mine."

The sincerity expressed in this connection bridged realms, merging the living with the deceased more seamlessly than ever before.

As the ghost began to fade into the night, a contented smile graced their translucent features. "Remember, every day offers a new voice to be heard and a new story to create. Share my truth; let it guide you through the shadows. Live your life unburdened by silence, open yourself to love, for it is the only antidote to regret."

In their departure, the ghost left behind a sparkle of lingering light, embedding the protagonist's heart with hope. The cemetery remained a backdrop of whispers where thick fog curled around the stones, yet the path forward had become clear. No longer did those shadows of regret feel like chains; instead, they transformed into gentle reminders, a roadmap leading to authenticity, courage, and connection. The protagonist took a deep breath, invigorated by the night. Reality's weight no longer felt burdensome, but rather like an invigorating breeze that filled their lungs with purpose. This encounter had ignited a fervent flame within the indomitable spirit of self-expression. They felt poised to step into the world and articulate their own truths, embrace their vulnerabilities, and lay bare their heart, ensuring that the echoes of regret would not weave through their life's narrative. With each step away from the gravestones, the protagonist understood that every relationship is colored by unspoken truths, dreams waiting to take flight, and love yearned to flourish. The lesson gleaned from the ghost would accompany them as they navigated the complexities of their own relationships, creating avenues for reconciliation and authenticity.

The journey was far from over, but the path was now illuminated, the whispers of the past merging harmoniously with newfound aspirations. As dawn approached, the protagonist cast one last glance back at the cemetery, the evidence of deep encounters that resonate across lifetimes. They took stock of the weight the ghost had lifted, an opportunity to embrace life beyond mere existence. And as they ventured out into the waking world, the essence of connection echoed within them, guiding each step toward a life filled with honesty, authenticity, and enduring love.

Lessons from the Beyond

As the protagonist meandered through the cemetery, the weight of the atmosphere thickened. The crisp air carried a sense of stillness, the kind that holds secrets begging to be uncovered. Each tombstone stood like a guardian of stories untold, waiting for someone to listen. It was here, amidst the weathered stones, that they would encounter not just the memories of the past, but the spirits who lived within them. Beneath the arching branches of an ancient oak tree, a faint glow flickered at the periphery of their vision. Drawn by an invisible tether, the protagonist approached.

As they neared the light, a figure began to take the shape of a woman, ethereal yet vibrant, dressed in the gown of another time. Her eyes sparkled with wisdom and mischief, evoking a sense of familiarity that sent a rush of warmth through the protagonist's heart.

"Welcome, dear traveler," she said. Her voice as soothing as a gentle breeze. "I am Clara, a keeper of tales."

The protagonist stood frozen, a myriad of emotions swirling within. "Who… Who are you?" they managed to ask.

"I am but a whisper among the graves, a bridge between life and what comes after. I have lived, I have loved, and now I share the lessons of existence with those who can still learn."

She took a step closer, her essence shimmering with an otherworldly glow. "Are you ready to listen?"

Nodding, the protagonist felt an inexplicable sense of trust envelop them. "Yes," they answered, heart racing with anticipation.

Clara's delicate hands animatedly gestured, drawing the protagonist's gaze to the neighboring graves. "Every spirit here carries a fragment of knowledge, a lesson crafted from the essence of their journey. I shall introduce you to a few."

With a wave of her hand, the surroundings shifted, unveiling the first ghost: a stout, jovial man, his laughter echoing softly in the air. He wore a thick beard, and his eyes sparkled like stars as he approached.

"I am Gregor," he proclaimed, an amiable smile stretching across his face. "I have lived my life in laughter, you see. My lessons are simple but vital: Do not take life too seriously. Embrace joy in the mundane."

The protagonist felt an immediate connection to Gregor's buoyant spirit. "But what about the pain? What of the heartache?"

Gregor chuckled, a rich, rumbling sound that seemed to resonate with the ground beneath them. "Ah, my friend! Pain is as much a part of life as laughter is. One cannot exist without the other. To cherish joy, we must also recognize sorrow. Instead of fearing the melancholy, dance with it. Allow it to teach you."

With that, a serene smile graced Gregor's lip. Somehow, his peace was infectious. The protagonist found solace in his words, an understanding that pain could coexist with joy, perhaps even enhance it. "Thank you, Gregor. I understand," the protagonist whispered, a spark igniting within them.

But Clara was already beckoning once more, guiding them to the next spirit. This time, a young woman appeared, her eyes captivating yet surrounded by a veil of sadness.

"Hello. I'm Lila," she said softly, uncertainty lacing her voice.

There was a gentle fragility about her, but an intensity that demanded attention. "Lila, what wisdom do you carry?" the protagonist asked, drawn to her enigmatic presence.

"In my life, I was consumed by a desire for acceptance," she confessed, her voice trembling. "I chased after the validation of others, often losing myself in the process. I thought that success and approval equated to love, but it was the opposite that I learned. True love comes from within."

She paused, her gaze anchoring the protagonist. "My lesson is to embrace who you are, wholly and fiercely. Do not bend your identity for others' approval. Find the strength within to stand tall, even when faced with judgment."

The protagonist's heart ached with empathy for Lila. Her words echoed the struggles they faced in their own life, the theater of expectations and the haunting fear of inadequacy. "But it's so easy to feel lost in the whirlwind of others' opinions," they murmured.

Lila's smile was faint but genuine. "It is in moments of silence, in the stillness between breaths, that you will find the truth. Listen to your own heart; it holds the compass to your journey. Love yourself unconditionally, for that is the legacy worth leaving behind."

As her spirit began to dissolve into the air, an overwhelming sense of gratitude washed over the protagonist. "Thank you, Lila," they whispered.

Once more, Clara's beckoning hand guided them forward, though this time the atmosphere shifted, crackling with energy. A tall, regal figure emerged. His presence commanding, wrapped in layers of purpose. "I am Leonardo," he declared, the gravitas of his voice reverberating through the air. "I sought wisdom through knowledge, decision-making abstract from matters of the heart. My lesson is that intellect alone cannot steer the ship of life."

"What do you mean?" the protagonist asked, curiosity piqued.

"While knowledge is crucial, it is the heart that leads us toward true fulfillment. We may understand the world through data and reasoning, but compassion and love color our existence. One may navigate through life's complexities with logic, yet without passion and connection, we remain but shadows of our potential."

The protagonist reflected on Leonardo's profound statement. There was a resonating truth in it that intellect could only take someone so far. "And what of those who fear vulnerability?" they inquired.

Leonardo's laughter was deep and resonant, rich with experience. "Ah, my friend, vulnerability is not weakness, it is strength! To share oneself authentically with others is to create bonds that surpass mortality. Love and connection are the true legacies we leave behind. Go forth and embrace both your intellect and heart; balance the two, and you will navigate the seas of life with grace."

With a nod of appreciation, the protagonist acknowledged Leonardo's wisdom. They were beginning to see the tapestry of spirit, teachings unfurl before them, intertwining and connecting with their own journey. Clara gently guided the protagonist further into the cemetery, leading them to a smaller gravestone, weathered yet dignified. A spirit emerged of an older woman; her face lined with kindness and experience. "Welcome, dear child," she greeted with a nurturing warmth. "I am Maura, and my life was adorned, though not without hardship. My lesson lies in acceptance, the acceptance of both joy and suffering."

The protagonist felt drawn to Maura's comforting presence. "How do we find acceptance?" they asked, yearning for guidance.

"Acceptance does not mean resignation," Maura explained gently.

"It means embracing what is real, even when it feels heavy. I watched many sunsets, and in each, I learned to release what I could not change. It is liberating! Cling not to the past, but find beauty in the present, however fleeting it may be."

Maura's words carried a weight that settled in the protagonist's heart. "But how can we let go when our hearts ache for what was?"

"The act of letting go is an art form," she smiled. "It demands patience, self-love, and willingness to be vulnerable with yourself. Honor your pain, but do not allow it to define you. You are the artist of your own life and can paint with the hues of acceptance, resilience, and love."

The protagonist wiped away tears that glistened in their eyes. "Thank you, Maura. I will strive to honor your teaching."

As the spirit of Maura began to shimmer away, the protagonist felt a surge of knowledge within them. Clara stood with approval in her eyes, nudging them to continue their exploration.

There was an extraordinary shift as they drew near a gravestone that pulsated with an iridescent light. A young boy appeared, perhaps no older than ten, with laughter twinkling in his eyes that refracted joy and wonder. "Hello!" he chirped, bouncing on the tips of his toes. "I'm Timmy!"

"Timmy," the protagonist smiled, "What do you want to share

with us today?"

"Life is a treasure hunt!" he exclaimed, exuberance spilling from every word. Every day is full of mysteries waiting for us to uncover. I learned that some of the best treasures are moments of laughter, joy, and sweet adventures. Chase those moments. They make the heart sing!"

The protagonist laughed, captivated by the young boy's spirit. "How do I chase them when life feels so heavy?"

Timmy's expression turned serious. "You must look for the small things! A butterfly, a laugh with a friend, the sun on your face! Life is not just the big things; it's also the tiny miracles hiding all around you. Imagine the joy of a treasure hunt!"

As the warmth of his contagious spirit enveloped the protagonist, a thought ignited within them, the realization that life's vibrancy resided in the simplest moments. "Thank you, Timmy! I will remember to seek the little joys in life," they replied, inspired by his wisdom.

With a wave of Clara's hand, the landscape shifted once more, revealing a spirit cloaked in tranquility, her face serene yet contemplative. "Greetings," she said softly, emanating a sense of calm that wrapped around the protagonist like a warm blanket. "I am Seraphina."

"Seraphina, your presence is calming," the protagonist noted with reverence. "What truths do you wish to impart?"

"My lesson revolves around patience," she shared. "In my years as a healer, I learned that everything unfolds in its own time. Humanity often rushes through life, chasing destinies that may not yet be ready for them."

The protagonist pondered this, recalling times they'd pushed against fate's current. "How can patience bring wisdom?" they inquired.

"Through patience, we learn to truly listen, both to ourselves and to the world around us," she replied. "In moments of stillness, revelations arise. Let the rhythms of life guide you. Embrace the journey, trust the process, and know that nothing is lost; everything happens as it should, in perfect timing."

It felt as if Seraphina had peeled back layers within the protagonist, revealing an understanding that peace could be found in acceptance and love, intertwined with the cadence of patience. "Thank you, Seraphina. Your wisdom resonates deeply," the protagonist acknowledged, feeling enriched by her presence.

As Clara led them onward, the protagonist felt the gathered wisdom transform into a quilt of understanding encompassing their heart for each lesson from the departed spirits resonating within. They were now more aware of how interconnected life truly was, how love persisted beyond the boundary of death.

Finally, Clara stopped before a gravestone adorned with wildflowers, vibrant and alive against the somber backdrop. The spirit that emerged was an elderly man with sparkling eyes that held stories untold. Salutations, seeker of truth, he greeted warmly. "I am Walter, and I have witnessed the dance of life from many angles."

"What do you want to share, Walter?" the protagonist asked, eager to hear his insights.

"I have learned that kindness is our greatest legacy," he replied, his voice rich with compassion. "In a world riddled with chaos, kindness pierces through darkness, guiding us to compassion for ourselves and for one another."

"How can kindness create a legacy?" the protagonist asked, intrigued.

Walter's smile grew as he continued, "Acts of kindness ripple through time. They create connections that transcend our physical existence. Each kindness has the power to inspire others to continue the chain, to spread love like seeds in the wind. It is how we embody love, how we cultivate our collective humanity."

Tears glistened in the protagonist's eyes as the weight of Walter's wisdom settled into their heart. Here, in this sanctuary of spirits, they felt the collective assurance that love and kindness formed the fabric of existence, unifying all lives. "Thank you, Walter. I will cultivate kindness in my life," they promised, deep gratitude swelling within.

As Clara watched the reunion of the protagonist with each spirit, her gentle smile mirrored the light they now carried in their soul. The journey had transformed them, filling their heart with lessons that transcended the boundaries of time and death. "You are not alone. Each encounter leaves a trace upon the heart," Clara remarked softly. "You are learning to carry these whispers forward, to listen, and to share."

"Do you feel it? The weight and the lightness all at once?" the protagonist asked, emotions swirling like leaves in an autumn breeze.

"Yes," Clara replied, her voice a gentle caress. "You carry the essence of those whose lives touched yours, and in so doing, you honor their existence, their love."

As the sun began to dip below the horizon, casting a golden hue across the cemetery, the protagonist felt a sense of completion, a restful embrace from the spirits that guided them. The wisdom imparted by each soul echoed within, carving pathways toward acceptance, love, and connection. With newfound clarity about their journey and the interconnectedness of existence, the protagonist stepped away from the graves, carrying not just the whispers of the past but a deeper understanding of the legacy they would create in life. In the world beyond, the spirits watched on, smiles touching their faces as a new voice began to emerge, one rooted in love, acceptance, and kindness, a voice that would whisper through the winds of time, reminding the living of the precious treasure contained within the shared stories of humanity. As the protagonist walked away, the weight of loss transformed into the gentle embrace of memory, and they knew they would carry the lessons learned into the world, nourished by the love of those who came before, chasing after the little joys and spreading kindness wherever they wandered. The journey was far from over; it had only just begun.

The Color of Memories

A Palette of Emotions

The world unfolded in an array of colors as the protagonist stepped beyond the mundane, entering a realm where memories danced vividly before their eyes. Each shade, each hue encapsulated an emotion, weaving a tapestry of feelings into the very fabric of the atmosphere, making the air shimmer with sentiment. The luscious greens whispered of nostalgia, while the fiery reds ignited passion and longing; each color held a story, a fragment of the protagonist's journey through life, loss, and love.

As they walked further into this vibrant landscape, the deep blues of sorrow and melancholy enveloped them like a familiar embrace. The protagonist stopped, captivated by the richness of this color, instantly transported back to the moment of their grandmother's passing. It was her favorite deep blue shawl, draped over her frail shoulders during the last few days nestled in her hospital bed. The memory flooded in, bringing with it an acute sense of longing. They could almost feel the chill of the hospital room, the thrum of machines in the background, and the weight of unspoken words lingering in the air.

Sinking into the memory, the protagonist recalled the sharp, sterile smells mingling with the scent of their grandmother's lavender perfume. That blue shawl was not just a garment; it was a vessel for comfort, an emblem of her warmth. It wrapped around memories, the laughter shared during Sunday dinners, the gentle touch of her hand while sharing stories of old, and her unwavering love that felt as deep and infinite as the ocean. As the protagonist allowed themselves to linger in this affection, the blue deepened, evoking the gentle waves of sorrow that washed over them, yet also a profound gratitude for the time they had shared.

Moving on, the protagonist discovered patches of soft yellow interspersed amongst the blue, bright and warm like sunlight streaming through clouds after a storm. It was the color of their childhood, moments spent in the embrace of friends, joyful laughter echoing in memory. They closed their eyes, inhaling the sweetness of that warmth, and instantly found themselves back at a sun-drenched picnic in the park, a birthday celebration filled with balloons, cake, and the shrieks of delight from children chasing each other in every direction. Yellow did not simply represent happiness; it embodied the carefree spirit of youth, the untainted joy of now. It was the color of every summer afternoon spent playing in the golden sunshine, the sensation of grass beneath their bare feet, and the taste of freshly squeezed lemonade. It was interwoven with the laughter of friends, the kind that rang loudly, filling the air, and spilling out into the world, untouched by the weight of adulthood.

The protagonist longed to chase that memory, who wouldn't want to bottle joy like that? Yet, in this kaleidoscope of emotions, deeper shades emerged colors so vibrant they pulsated with energy, hues that echoed life's complexity. They felt an intoxicating crimson, fierce and overwhelming, representing both love and anger. The red glowed around memories of their first love, an experience that was as thrilling as it was painful. They remembered the electric pulse of affection that rushed through their veins, a dance of stolen kisses under the stars, the flutter of butterflies in their stomach, and the vulnerable hollowness of heartbreak when it all came crashing down.

The protagonist's heart raced as memories surfaced, fights fueled by pride, passionate reconciliations, and nights spent tangled in conversation that stretched far into the dawn. Each memory painted an intricate relationship, a mixture of sweetness and bitterness that ebbed and flowed, much like the color of love itself. And though tinged with shades of anger, the brightness of the experience reminded them of the rawness of feeling deeply, of allowing oneself to be completely open, to risk it all for the sake of connection.

Amidst this exploration, the protagonist stumbled upon the purples of introspection, deep and contemplative, enigmatic in its nature. These shades summoned memories of quiet evenings spent with a journal, pouring over thoughts and feelings that ebbed and flowed like the tides. It pulled them into the depths of self-discovery, moments spent deciphering who they were, what they desired, and the paths they chose. There were evenings of solitude wrapped in those purple hues, sipping herbal tea while the world outside moved incessantly.

These colors reflected the essence of learning and unlearning: grappling with uncomfortable truths, acknowledging fears, and pinning hopes for the future. They expressed the mixed emotions of joy and distress with the same intensity, a longing to grow, yet the fear of what that growth might entail. The protagonist reveled in the possibilities each shade offered, recognizing the importance of exploring not just the surface but the rich layers beneath. As they wandered through this metaphorical garden of colors, vibrant shades began to bleed into one another, creating beautiful gradients the blending of tears and laughter, heartache and healing. A sunset hue enveloped them with its melancholic beauty and fragile warmth. Here lay the artistry of life, how joy and sadness coexisted, how one painted the vibrancy of the other, and how each moment was a brushstroke contributing to a larger masterpiece. Emerging at the intersection of colors, the protagonist stumbled upon the theme of loss; a sepia-toned brown whispered stories of memories past, housing the grittiness of life, the bittersweet nature of letting go. In this color, they remembered their beloved grandfather, whose passing had cast shadows of sorrow that felt insurmountable at times. They recalled his wise words, "We may leave this world, but we do not disappear." The richness of this memory lay not only in the tints of mourning but in the lessons imparted. The protagonist could see their grandfather sitting in his old armchair, telling tales of his youth, tales of love and loss intertwined within every story.

Through the sepia tone conveyed by a mixture of love, longing, and cherished friendship, the protagonist was reminded that loss is a testament to the love experienced. Just as colors blended to form new shades, so too did memories intertwine, creating narratives woven through laughter, shared tears, and cherished moments. They took a step back, taking in the palette that surrounded them. Each color, each memory, stood out boldly against the canvas of existence an ongoing masterpiece that continued to evolve with each experience.

Here, colors were more than mere visuals; they served as emotional containers through which the protagonist connected with the essence of their life, each shade enriching their understanding of who they were, one intricately built from moments of sorrow, joy, love, and longing. As they reflected on their relationship with color, a deeper understanding emerged. Colors served as vessels, creating bridges that crossed the chasm of time, linking past experiences with present emotions. The protagonist realized how these colors returned in rhythm with certain smells, sights, or sounds they encountered in their daily life.

Their favorite blue dress hung in the closet, and with every glance, they recalled the warmth of friendship resonating in every memory tied to it. Running their fingers over fabric that contained meaningful hues became an act of honoring the stories tied to it. They found themselves considering how everyday moments carried emotional weight, how each color stirred something profound and fundamental within. The sunny yellows of morning light spilling through their window felt different than those seen through a dusty pane. It was a messenger, a nudging reminder of countless sunrises spent dreaming about possibilities, the anticipation each day carried.

The protagonist recognized the beauty in these fleeting instances; moments that seemed benign were woven through every change in hue, each telling a story of human experience. In an age where emotions often felt bottled up or sugar-coated, the protagonist longed to share this palette of emotions with others to paint their experiences as vivid as colors blossoming in a garden awaiting spring. Memories were meant to be expressed, shared, and felt deeply, for they encompassed the human condition in all its fractal beauty, where acceptance of loss quelled sorrow and joy became a luminescent experience.

In this vibrant world, they envisioned a canvas spreading before them, a personal mural composed of distinct colors threaded with nuances of emotion, each stroke intentional in its placement. Each color spoke of loss and remembrance, of moments held secretly, where love transcended time and space. This tapestry became a collective narrative of joy, sorrow, hope, and triumph, evidence to human resilience that could withstand storms of disappointment and be illuminated by warmth and connection.

With renewed intention, the protagonist thought of sharing this vision more widely. They envisioned gatherings in which friends and family came together to explore their collective palettes, creating a grand tapestry of memories merging with life stories. Such a space could encourage authenticity, catalyze compassion, and generate conversations that celebrated the intertwining of happiness and sorrow. As they contemplated the possibilities, the protagonist clenched a small stone colored gentle amber, its warmth resting comfortably in their palm. They could feel the warmth of gratitude emanating from it, an anchor in understanding how each color, how every emotion could flow freely. It reminded them of autumn afternoons spent with loved ones, laughing amidst fallen leaves, rooted in connection and appreciation for the present. Perhaps this was the essence of life embracing and celebrating each color, each story creating a more vibrant self.

Moving toward the horizon of this colorful journey, the protagonist felt a swell of resolve. They recognized that while each color had its own story, they were always interconnected. The deep blues of sorrow mingled effortlessly with the yellows of joy, while the purples of introspection intertwined with the fiery reds of love. Embracing this intricate dance of colors created a spectrum reflecting the complexity of existence.

Upon returning from this vivid exploration, the protagonist carried each memory and emotion, vivid and alive, into the world outside. They felt empowered, ready to paint their journey boldly, to honor every color for what it represented. Their heart brimmed with gratitude for the connective threads that wound through every member of their family, thankful for the colors they contributed to their existence. In that vibrant palette of emotions, they understood that life would inevitably consist of contrasts, each moment a new brushstroke adding volume and depth, culminating into a masterpiece meant to be shared.

As they stepped back into their everyday life, the protagonist took a deep breath, their vision rich with the stories they would one day tell. It was an invitation to embrace the full spectrum of human experience, to recognize colors not only as fragments of memory but as guides illuminating the paths of the heart and a reminder of the beauty in the interplay of life.

Blending the Past and Present

The air was thick with the scent of blooming jasmine and freshly cut grass as the protagonist stepped deeper into the vibrant landscape of memories. Each color before them pulsed with life, bright hues interweaving like notes in a symphony. The blues sang of laughter shared on sunlit days, while the reds resonated with the fervor of love's embrace. Yet, within this kaleidoscope, shadows lingered a muted gray, a deep crimson, a tarnished gold, echoes of sorrow that melded with the vibrancy of joy, creating a tapestry rich with complexity.

As they walked through this colorful wonderland, the protagonist felt a magnetic pull to the swells and troughs of their emotional palette. They paused beside an enormous canvas, its colors swirling together like a storm in a painter's mind. This was not merely a representation of moments lived; it was a reflection of all the vibrant experiences that shaped their existence, woven together with delicate threads of loss and triumph. With a steady hand, the protagonist took a brush, dipping it into the brilliant yellow that radiated warmth. They remembered the laughter of childhood, moments spent chasing fireflies on warm summer nights, the exhilaration that filled their heart as they caught one. Yet, woven into this vivid yellow were streaks of gray shadows of memories laced with the absence of those who had nurtured them during those carefree days. The strokes of gray whispered of loss, of cherished voices now silenced, reminding them that joy often danced in tandem with sorrow. Each color they blended told a story.

As they added a splash of soft lavender, a hue that signified tranquility. The protagonist was transported to a moment of quiet reflection in their grandmother's garden. The lush flowers, once alive with their grandmother's tender care, now existed only in fading memories, buried beneath the weight of regret for time unspent. Yet, amidst that sorrow, the gentle lavender reminded them of the lessons learned under the shade of her wisdom, the quiet strength that lingered long after her voice faded.

As they continued to mix colors, the protagonist began to see the beauty in blending the vibrancy of joy with the depths of grief. They dipped their brush into a bold crimson, representing love, unyielding and fierce. Suddenly, a flash of memory sparked; they recalled standing in the kitchen, flour dust swirling through the air, laughter bubbling as they baked cookies side by side with a beloved friend who had since passed. The sweetness of those moments, now ripe with nostalgia, was tinged with the bittersweet knowledge of absence. The love they shared existed in joy but was tinged with loss, each bite of a cookie brought forth a wave of remembrance, sweet and sorrowful.

The protagonist recognized that the power of memory lay not in erasing the pain but in holding it alongside the joy. It was like painting the sky at sunset, where the brilliance of the oranges and golds surrendered to twilight's deep blues and blacks all the while, coexisting to create breathtaking beauty. They stepped back to observe the canvas. The landscape of their life unfolded before them like a story told in color. Each stroke represented a moment; some blended easily, intertwining seamlessly, while others clashed, bold and stark against their surroundings. That contrast was not to be shunned. Instead, it was to be celebrated each moment, joyous or painful, had shaped who they were.

In that revelation, the protagonist felt a new kind of growth surge through their being. To honor their full narrative was to acknowledge the intricate interplay of experience. It was like walking on a tightrope stretched between two extremes, joy and grief, laughter and tears and recognizing that the distance between those poles was not a chasm to be avoided but a bridge to be crossed. The watercolors continued to blend, forming unforeseen shades. A deep teal emerged, representing those moments of profound solitude that allowed reflection and growth. There were times when solitude turned into overcast clouds days when the loneliness felt overwhelming. Yet, as the colors mingled, new life emerged from the depths, enriching the canvas and unveiling a vibrant emerald, an emblem of renewal and rebirth.

The protagonist realized the importance of nurturing these emotions and allowing them to coexist. Just as one wouldn't discard the brushstrokes left behind by the artist, they too must keep intact their memories both the brightest and darkest moments that constituted their experience. The gray brushstrokes didn't diminish the beauty of the rainbow; rather, they gave it depth, presence, and meaning. Without them, the vibrancy would be merely surface level, a two-dimensional illustration devoid of a soul.

As the afternoon light began to soften, the protagonist sensed the urgency of their task. They continued to mix colors fervently, their strokes growing bolder with conviction. The canvas came alive, pulsating with energy, each layer telling tales of resilience nurtured amidst pain, of friendships forged through adversity, of love wrapping around loss like a comforting embrace. Then, they dipped the brush into a rich gold, a symbol of wisdom and insight. Memories of family gatherings, laughter around the dinner table, and quiet moments shared over cups of tea rose to the surface. Each moment felt like gold dust, shimmering amid the chaos, those specks glimmering as reminders of the treasure trove of bonds created over a lifetime.

Yet, even in this place of warmth, the protagonist noticed a dark hue creeping in, a reflection of the struggles faced in relationships arguments, misunderstandings, and the haunting echo of words left unspoken. Those moments, too, deserved attention. As painful as they might have been, they taught valuable lessons about vulnerability, forgiveness, and understanding. Acknowledging these truths allowed space for healing, inviting the brightness of those golden memories to shine even more radiantly against the backdrop of tumult.

As the protagonist continued to apply the layers of color, they began to see not just their own story but the interconnectedness of experiences with others. How the palette of their life blended with those around them: family, friends, lovers, mentors. Each relationship infused their colors with new meanings, nuances that were uniquely theirs yet shared, creating a generational tapestry rich with echoes of connection. The protagonist considered those before them, ancestors they'd never met but felt deep within. How their stories were painted onto this canvas, too. A fierce woman who stood against the odds, unyielding even in heartbreak. A tender man who taught the importance of kindness amidst adversity. Their legacies were etched through vibrant colors, and with each brush stroke, the protagonist honored their attempts to integrate those narratives into their own life. At that moment, realization struck like thunder. This blending of the past and present represented not just acceptance but a profound respect for all parts of oneself. It was essential to remember that pain and joy coexist in life's richest tapestry. To admit that loss would not erase love; rather, grief could deepen the appreciation for the moments of light that had come before.

As the sun dipped below the horizon, its rays filtered through the colors on the canvas, casting a dreamy glow. The protagonist stepped back, allowing the full view to wash over them. The amalgamation of vibrant memories intertwined with the shadows of pain formed a breathtaking landscape. Each color poured into another, creating boundaries that faded, thus embodying the beautifully fluid nature of experience. In that canvas, they found a powerful affirmation: that life was never merely a collection of separate moments. It was about holding space for everything, the colors of joy and the smudges of pain, the shimmering golds of love alongside the muted tones of loss. It was about weaving those shades into the narrative of existence and allowing them to coexist as nestled partners, eternally intertwined.

With arms wide open, the protagonist recognized the fundamental truth that every stroke added to the richness of their character. It had taken time, reflection, and acceptance to navigate the complexities of their emotions, but at last, they stood before a vivid representation of their life, offering a glimpse into the resilience that emerged from amalgamating the past with the present. And in that moment of synthesis, they whispered a silent pledge to honor every aspect of their story to carry forth the joy and to embrace the pain as part of what made them whole. Each brush stroke stood as a witness to living, to experiencing to feeling deeply and passionately. The journey ahead would continue to bring new colors for the canvas. With the knowledge that blending the past with the present was a sacred art, they were ready. In the depths of their being, a profound sense of wholeness settled, a knowing realization that embracing the entirety of life both joy and grief created not just a beautiful narrative but an enduring legacy, a living testament of the power inherent in the human experience.

With that sense of completeness encircling their heart, the protagonist turned away from the canvas, ready now to face the world anew, vibrant and whole.

The Vibrancy of Love

The moment the protagonist stepped into the sun-drenched clearing, the colors enveloped them like a warm embrace, wrapping them in a cocoon of nostalgia and serenity. It was a world where memories danced on the breeze, where each hue shimmered with significance. Amidst the swirling palette of vibrant greens and earthy browns, there was a burst of pink that caught their eye a vibrant, deep pink that called to them like the heartbeat of a long-lost friendship. Intrigued, they drew closer, feeling a magnetic pull toward this emblem of love.

As they approached the cluster of pink blooms swaying gently in the breeze, memories flooded their mind, exquisite and overwhelming in their clarity. Each flower seemed to whisper secrets of days gone by, invoking moments steeped in warmth and laughter. They could almost hear the laughter of loved ones who had passed, echoing through the petals, intertwining with the sweet scent of the blossoms. One flower in particular, a vivid peony seemed to stand out among the rest. It beckoned them closer, and as they knelt down, the protagonist felt as if they were transported to a cherished moment from their childhood. They could see their grandmother's garden, the air thick with the fragrance of countless blooms, and hear the cheerful songs that filled the afternoon air as family gathered to celebrate life, love, and connection.

"Your eyes light up like these flowers," their grandmother used to say, her voice imbued with love. "Whenever you smile, everything around you burst into color."

The protagonist inhaled sharply as a wave of bittersweet emotion washed over them. It was in this garden that the essence of love had first taken root in their heart. Here, colors represented not just emotion, but a vivid landscape of shared experiences, a canvas painted with the brushstrokes of those who had come before. Memories unfolded before them like petals revealing their core, reminding them that love was never truly lost; it merely transformed, shifting in form and presence. They closed their eyes, and with each breath, they felt the whispers of those they had loved and lost. Their mother's laughter resonated, the way it used to echo in the household during evening dinners filled with warmth and banter. The smell of her favorite lavender soap filled their senses, a lingering reminder of her gentle touch as she tucked them in at night. That lavender, now tinged with the pink of happy memories, coiled around their heart, tethering them to the essence of love that echoed through time. With every inhalation, they remembered holidays spent in the company of those nearest to their heart, grandparents recapping old stories, aunts and uncles beneath starry skies, siblings creating mischief in sunlit afternoons. Each recollection was as vibrant as the blossoms surrounding them, embodying a warmth that sparked joy amid the melancholy shadow of their absence.

As the protagonist wandered deeper into the clearing, the vivid pink morphed into all shades of love: soft pastels embodying tender affection, vibrant hues encapsulating passion, and deep magentas representing steadfast commitment. They were reminded of how these colors of love shaped them, the friendships that had built their character, the romantic connections that stretched their hearts, and the powerful bonds of family that stitched the fabric of their identity. It became clear that love flourished even within the depth of grief; it existed within the unbroken cycles of life and death, weaving a tapestry of connections that persisted over time.

The vibrant pinks encapsulated all that love had been and would continue to be. With newfound clarity, the protagonist realized that embracing these memories was akin to nurturing a garden; all the love from those they had lost nurtured new growth within their own heart.

Love was like a great vine, twisting and turning, growing lush and strong, embedding itself deeper into their core with each shared moment. Just as each flower sprang from the earth, so too did new relationships emerge from the fertile soil of old connections, cultivated by the wisdom of the past and the lessons of love.

They opened their eyes, steadying themselves as they stood amidst the pink blooms. Each petal was like a reminder, illuminating the potency of their experiences. It was a heartfelt knowing that the essence of love never truly faded. Instead, it transformed like the changing seasons, creating new opportunities for connection while retaining the vitality of what had come before.

As they wandered further, the protagonist began to notice how this reverence for past relationships illuminated their current connections. They recalled a recent encounter with a dear friend; the heart-to-heart conversation had been filled with vulnerability and laughter. That friend's presence reminded them of the warmth radiating from the vibrant pink blossoms. The protagonist recognized how loving openly and honestly allowed them to carry the essence of those who had passed into their living experience.

With every interaction, they invited a spark of the love that had shaped them, threading it into the beautiful tapestry of their relationships. The absence of their loved ones felt less suffocating when they saw the world through the lens of gratitude. Rather than remain in a shadowed past, they began to bask in the radiant hues of joy, a reminder that love would always provide a beacon, guiding them through the darkness of grief and loss. The garden teemed with life, a visual and visceral representation of their vibrant memories.

Bees flitted between flowers, their busy buzz transforming into gentle reminders that just as they formed communities, so too could the protagonist embrace connection in all its forms. They were not alone, and neither were the manifestations of love that shaped who they had become.

Soon, the protagonist found themselves talking to the pink

blooms, sharing stories of loved ones lost and memories cherished, allowing their feelings to flow like an unbroken stream.

"Thank you," they whispered to the flowers, "for reminding me that love transforms. For illuminating each path I walk, filled with those who have left marks on my heart."

As the sun began to set, casting golden rays over the vibrant garden, the protagonist felt a sense of renewal wash over them. They marveled at how those they held close had inspired their journey; even from beyond the vibrant pinks blossomed as a testament to a bond that could withstand time, transcending the earthly plane to create a legacy of love.

With a heart full of appreciation, the protagonist turned to leave, but not without first tracing a path formed of colors in their mind pinks blooming in memory, trailing toward future loves yet unformed. They would plant seeds in their own garden, nurturing new relationships while honoring the essence of those who had come before them. Love was alive, and it would continue to shape their journey, blossoming anew with each memory embraced and cherished. The garden became a sacred space, where grief transformed into gratitude, sadness into joy, and loss into growth a vibrant proof that love, in all its shades and forms, never truly fades. It lives on in the hearts and minds of those left behind, watering the roots of connection that extend beyond the confines of mortality.

As the protagonist walked away, they felt imbued with the strength of love, ready to forge new connections while keeping the memories of the past vivid in the colors of their heart.

Ember of Traditions

Rituals of Remembrance

The living room was cloaked in a gentle hush, a reverent atmosphere enveloping the space as the protagonist and their family members gathered to honor a beloved figure, a matriarch whose spirit had woven the fabric of their shared lives. The familiar scent of sandalwood incense mingled with the faint aroma of freshly baked bread that wafted from the kitchen, wrapping everyone in a warm embrace of nostalgia. It wasn't just the smells that filled the air; the soft crackling of the fire in the hearth harmonized with whispered stories and the occasional laughter that punctuated the somber mood, creating a symphony of remembrance.

As the protagonist scanned the room, they noticed the customary family altar constructed atop an aged wooden table. Framed photographs, each a portal to the past, told tales of joyous celebrations and quiet moments of tenderness. The centerpiece was a simple yet elegant bouquet of white lilies, symbolizing purity and renewal. Each bloom seemed to reach out, drawing together the echoes of lives lived and loved, mingling grief with gratitude. The protagonist felt the weight of this gathering, an emotional tide that surged through the room. They glanced around at the faces of family members, some familiar, some tired from the weight of loss, yet each bearing the shared responsibility of keeping their loved one's spirit alive. Children, with their bright eyes and innocent smiles, brought a sense of lightness to the proceedings, reminding the adults that life, even amidst sadness, was still a celebration.

The protagonist's heart swelled with both sorrow and gratitude as they prepared to engage in the rituals that had become a cornerstone of their family traditions.

"Let's begin," their father said, his voice steady but laced with emotion. Each word held the significance of years spent remembering and honoring those who had passed before them. The act itself held power; it transformed ordinary elements into sacred symbols that connected generations.

As family members took their places, each carrying a small token or memory to share, the protagonist felt a sense of unity, a tapestry of threads binding them all in their shared history. The protagonist picked up a small wooden box, intricately carved and worn from years of use. Inside lay a collection of personal items that spoke volumes without uttering a word. A silver locket containing a photograph of their departed grandmother. A well-loved book of poetry, pages yellowed and dog-eared, gifted by a first love. A simple stone smooth and cool to the touch that had been carried for years as a talisman of courage. Holding these items felt like grasping fragments of an eternal bond.

As family members shared their tokens, the atmosphere shifted, becoming a landscape rich with memory and meaning. The protagonist's uncle lifted a vibrant scarf, its colors as bright as his memories.

"She wore this the last family reunion we had. I can still hear her laughter echoing, bridging the distance of time. Whenever I see this scarf, I'm reminded of that warmth."

The room nodded in understanding, acknowledging the significance of stories tied to physical objects. One by one, family members relayed their connection, sparking a dialogue that flowed freely. They recounted favorite memories: shared meals adorning the table, summer afternoons spent in the garden, lessons learned during quiet evenings spent reading together. Without realizing it, they were constructing a collective mosaic of remembrance, bound by love's unyielding threads woven through time.

After the sharing, the protagonist's mother suggested a moment of silence. They all closed their eyes, collectively holding their breath as if to suspend time itself. It felt as though they were reaching through the veil, honoring the presence of their departed loved one, seeking solace in the bonds formed and strengthened by love. Tears spilt into the quietness, a cleansing cascade of emotions that soothed the rawness of grief. With each droplet, the protagonist felt the space around them shift a release, a tribute; an acknowledgment of the pain they all carried yet chose to face together. This shared vulnerability was as much a part of their culture as the stories they told, a quiet testament to resilience amidst the fragility of life.

As laughter broke the silence, it became clear that even within sorrow, they possessed the ability to embrace joy. The protagonist was reminded of how traditions developed, shifting from solemn ceremonies to joyous gatherings. This ritual was a dance uniting love and loss, hilarity and heartache, a cycle that repeated itself through seasons and generations.

Next, family members moved to the kitchen where the smell of the tangy-sweet fruit punch prepared for the occasion beckoned them. Together, they poured the brightly colored liquid into glasses, echoing laughter and chatter as they toiled under the warm glow of dimmed lights. Here, the protagonist felt the atmosphere transform into something palpable every clink of the glass resonated with collective remembrance, each sip a reminder of sweetness shared and a life celebrated. Each shared sip of fruit punch was laced with stories of family traditions, their ancestors' journeys, hardships, triumphs, and tears.

"The stories remind us, keep us grounded, don't they?" the protagonist mused. They understood in their heart that traditions serve as mile markers in a long, winding road, guiding family members back to the essence of their shared lineage, reinforcing their connection by honoring their forbearer. As the night wore on, the protagonist's grandmother stepped forward to retrieve a handmade blanket from the back of the old couch. Soft and patchwork, it was a family creation, stitched together by hands of both the living and those now gone.

"This blanket has wrapped our family through joy and sorrow. It has seen births, deaths, and every significant moment in between," she said, laying it on the floor.

The idea sparked excitement. One by one, family members joined them on the floor, each nesting into the folds of the heirloom blanket, feeling how the threads awash in color intertwined with their own lives. The protagonist felt an overwhelming sense of belonging; it was as if every laugh and tear had been captured, every cherished memory woven into the fabric of their being.

Someone initiated a round of sharing why they felt grateful for their departed loved one, what they learned, and how those lessons translated into everyday life. The responses illuminated the circle like flickers of warmth igniting the dark. The protagonist listened intently, heartstrings tugged by each unique reflection the humility of a life lived with purpose, the importance of nurturing one another, and an unwavering faith in the power of love. Their aunt shared a particularly poignant story from the past. Touching on the cumbersome moments influenced by grief and loss, she described a pot of soup that sustained their family during difficult times. "That soup was everything during our hardest days. We passed it around the table, each of us taking turns adding ingredients based on our moods. Each bowl was a reminder of resilience."

The protagonist mused on how these rituals created bridges across generations. Not just about remembrance but renewal the participants were bonding over collective grief yet emphasizing moments of love, hope, and unity. Their family tree, with its many branches, stood resilient, nurtured by rituals that kept memories fresh, and their connections intertwined.

The evening culminated with the lighting of candles. Each family member held a small candle, flickering flames illuminating the faces of those present, casting shadows that resembled the spirits of the ancestors watching over them. They surrounded the altar, paying tribute as they offered silent prayers or shouted affirmations toward the sky, sending love to the stars where they believed their loved ones resided.

When the sun began setting, the soft glow of candlelight illuminated the protagonist's realization of the evening's significance. As they gazed at their family, they understood that these rituals were far more than mere actions they were lifelines thrown into the abyss of grief, vessels of connection that transported stories from one generation to the next. Each ritual reaffirmed the promise they made to never let the light of their loved one's fade. The protagonist felt the weight of history rest on their shoulders, ignited by their promise to carry forth the traditions that anchored their family. They recognized that while some bonds may be broken by death, the threads of memory are eternally mended through the rituals of remembrance, a sacred craft passed down with each generation destined to follow.

With midnight approaching, the protagonist's heart was filled with a profound sense of peace. The evening didn't erase the pain of loss but rather enriched it with the harrowing beauty of love that lingered. They understood now just how essential it was to keep those connections alive, to honor the past while embracing the present.

As they blew out the candles, the family whispered a collective promise into the night, knowing that the love they shared would echo onward, resurrected anew through the traditions of remembrance. There, within the heart of their living room, surrounded by the warmth of family, the protagonist grasped their role in this tapestry and committed to weaving their own stories into the traditions that would continue to guide future generations, igniting a lasting light in the hearts of all.

The Comfort of Shared Stories

The living room was filled with the rich aroma of freshly baked bread, mingling with the faint scent of lavender from the candles flickering in the corners. Outside, the evening sky gradually transformed into a canvas of deep oranges and soft purples, casting a warm glow through the window. Within this comforting space, the air thrummed with the light hum of conversation. Family members gathered together, each bringing their own stories, memories, and laughter to the table, creating an atmosphere that welcomed reminiscence and connection.

As the protagonist settled into their seat, they looked around at the faces of loved ones, each etched with both joy and sorrow. These were the people who had shared in their journey, who had walked alongside them through years of tumult and triumph alike. Tonight, they would honor the life of a cherished family member who had recently passed, weaving a tapestry of memory that might soften the edges of grief with the warmth of love. Time seemed to hold its breath for a moment before someone broke the silence, sharing a treasured memory. Laughter erupted, the kind of laughter that feels as though it echoes through the very walls of the room.

Grandmother Edna, with her mischievous eyes and a smile that seemed to light up the dim space, began to recount a tale from their childhood. Remember the summer when we tried to make lemonade from scratch? She laughed, shaking her head as if trying to shake off the years. The room buzzed with nods of recognition as those present, leaned in. "We ended up pouring too much sugar into that batch. I think we almost needed a dentist after that!"

The protagonist could envision that summer day, the sun shining down on their laughter-filled attempts to mix flavors, accidentally creating a concoction best described as an explosion of sweetness. Stories like these bounced joyfully from one person to another, stitching memories together, each thread colored by unique experiences. The protagonist watched and listened as anecdotes unfolded moments of laughter that were as sacred as the tears shed for the absence of their loved one. It was clear that in these shared stories, the family was not just preserving memories but also manifesting a sense of belonging amidst the heaviness of loss.

While the memories flowed freely, they often danced between laughter and sorrow, creating a beautiful collocation. Uncle Joe, known for his knack for comedic timing, stood to share his favorite experience with the departed elder.

"You know, she always claimed to have the greenest thumb in town," he began, a twinkle in his eye, "and yet, I remember the time she decided to grow tomatoes inside the house, the kitchen turned into a jungle. We almost had to fight our way out just to get to the fridge!"

The room erupted once again, laughter mixing seamlessly with the bittersweet remembrance of how their loved one delighted in the absurdity of life. These shared recollections illuminated the fact that mourners are not alone in their sorrow; the act of storytelling forged an invisible bond, knitting them closer together in their shared experiences of love and loss.

With each tale told, the protagonist felt the weight of grief begin to lighten, if only momentarily, by the joy they found within the memories that were brought to life.

The evening began to draw in, and the stories became more reflective, inviting deeper connections. Cousin Sarah, with her thoughtful gaze, shared a poignant memory, one that reverberated through the room with an ethereal quiet. "I remember her sitting by the window, reading to us from that old, worn book filled with fairy tales. It was magical, the way the stories would unfold, and she would always pause right at the best part.

Her voice trembled slightly as she continued, "After she finished reading, we would talk about our dreams and wishes, our hearts open and hopeful, listening as she encouraged us never to let those dreams fade."

There seemed to be an unspoken understanding that while storytelling held space for both light and dark, it also honored the lives lost by invoking the vibrancy of the relationships that had shaped their collective identities. With every story shared, they were reminded not just of the departed's absence, but of the enduring legacy left behind in the hearts of those who remained. Each thread woven into the fabric of their gathering helped them to remember that love, while often punctuated by loss, could also provide solace and continuity.

As the waves of reminiscence washed over the room, the conversation flowed naturally, exposing deeper layers of meaning and connection. Aunt Claire, her voice, steady yet saturated with emotion, offered a story that spoke directly to the heart of what it means to grapple with the duality of joy and grief. "That time we all went camping by the lake...," she started, her eyes flickering as she recalled the bittersweet memory. "The storm came out of nowhere, and we all thought we were going to drown in our tents!"

She paused for effect, allowing laughter to ripple through the group before adding, "But what I remember most is how we huddled together, telling ghost stories and singing songs, the uncertainty and fear turned into a celebration of being together. Through Aunt Claire's story, the protagonist recognized a profound truth: the ways in which laughter and vulnerability were interwoven within their family tradition were essential in processing grief. It highlighted the reality that while they mourned the physical absence of their loved one, they could still honor their spirit through the very act of gathering. In those moments of shared laughter, a glimpse of their loved one's essence would emerge, reminding them of the joy she brought to their lives.

As the storytelling continued to flourish like blossoms in spring, the protagonist felt a strong desire to participate. They took a deep breath, summoning the courage needed to share their own memory. "I remember the way she would always make us pancakes on Sunday mornings, how the kitchen would be filled with laughter and the smell of syrup. I can still hear her saying, 'A little more butter never hurt anyone!'"

Their voice wavered but strengthened with the warmth of the memory. That simple, loving act transformed into a lasting tradition, one that perpetuated itself even now. The protagonist felt a deep sense of connection with the family as they recounted how love could be found in the simplest of gestures, reinforced through storytelling that filled the gaps of their collective memory. The room fell silent momentarily, a sacred pause hanging in the air as each person reflected on their loved one through the lens of their instincts and feelings. It was an acknowledgment of love's enduring presence, even amid the eyebrows raised, the laughter shared, and the tears unspilled.

Uncle Joe chimed in, his voice softer now, weaving in a sense of connection to the departed, "You know, it's funny. I think she had a knack for turning the ordinary into something magical. I remember she took us to that rundown carnival."

The words flowed effortlessly as he recounted an adventure where joy erupted like popcorn kernels in hot oil, where they rode rides that were perhaps not as safe as they should have been but were filled with giggles and glee. By sharing stories that echoed through the rooms, woven together like threads in a quilt, the family acknowledged the uniqueness of their shared experience. It became apparent that storytelling nurtured healing, creating a collective presence that brought forth a sense of community within the walls.

This realization resonated deeply with the protagonist, igniting a fire of understanding that grief, though isolating at times, could be softened through family stories. The heart of the gathering, laughter began to intertwine with tears; both were just as valid, both were reflections of love and their pledge to keep memories alive. Stories illuminated their journey as they carved out a new narrative, one that embraced the complexities of life including its joys and sorrows. As the evening wore on, the stories became more vibrant, like colors spilled across a lovely canvas. The room exploded with spirited anecdotes filled with double extenders, exaggerated claims, and delightful twists that made the protagonist want to laugh and cry simultaneously. They realized that this joyous mingling of memory created a patchwork quilt of familial identity, with each story acting as a stitch that bound them closer together.

As they listened to tales of adventures, mistakes, and unyielding resilience, the protagonist recognized that these stories were essential, each reflected facets of their shared experiences. It became evident that the act of storytelling created avenues for understanding and empathy, allowing them to navigate through their emotions. They could endure the weight of loss yet still feel hope carried within the echoes of laughter. A song, bright and buoyant in nature, arose from the back of the room as Grandma Edna began humming an old tune, her voice carrying warmth rich and deep, just as it had in the past.

Suddenly, that hum transformed into joyous choral tones, everyone chiming in an impromptu celebration of life and legacy. As they sang, the protagonist reflected on the way this experience had transcended mere words, as if the melodies woven through their stories were an embodiment of love itself. It was a space less moment where laughter intertwined with grief, where memory etched itself deeply into the hearts of those present, creating threads of connection that shimmered like golden rays breaking through an overcast sky. The stories continued to flow, unrushed and organic, illuminating the lessons learned from the past through humor and vulnerability. In the midst of laughter, tears often pooled in the corners of eyes. Those silent exchanges held strength in their fragility, but also power as they embodied the connections they cherished. With each tale, it became increasingly clear that storytelling was not simply about preserving memories; it was an act of loving those who came before. It was an acknowledgment of how the past shaped their present and a promise to carry the legacies forward.

As the night wore on, the protagonist felt an overwhelming sense of gratitude toward those gathered around them. Together, they built a space where joy could blossom despite the heaviness of grief. It struck them deeply that their collective memory was evidence to the human experience, fragile yet steadfast. The evening could have lingered beyond the hour, with stories floating upon the air like fairy dust, enchanting and liberating.

But as the last echoes of laughter faded, a soft silence filled the room, a silence not steeped in sorrow but rather a gentle acceptance of shared grief and unwavering love. The protagonist absorbed the power of the moment, recognizing that those shared narratives, both humorous and heart-wrenching, served as threads binding their familial tapestry. Each recollection contributed to the identity of the family, a living history that would carry forth their loved one's legacy, long after they were gone.

In those moments, the protagonist also made a silent promise: to keep sharing these stories, to honor the threads of love that anchored them to one another, to weave a fabric that reflected the essence of joy and sorrow in unison. From this day forward, they would wield the gift of storytelling, intertwining memories into the very fabric of their own life, ensuring that love flourishes amid the flames of grief. The gathering slowly began to disperse, but the ambiance of connection remained.

Members embraced one another, exchanging knowing glances, smiles that reflected understanding without words. The protagonist walked toward the door; their heart buoyed by the warmth of shared stories that filled the air. It was a poignant reminder of how in mourning, laughter could coexist beautifully with tears, and through storytelling, the bonds of love and memory could turn grief into something brighter, marking the beginning of a new chapter in their narrative. The quiet aftermath of the gathering, the protagonist took a moment to reflect. They would carry these stories with them, into new circles of friendship, into future gatherings where laughter and warm embraces would follow tales shared. In honoring the departed's memory, they would nurture the connections that shaped not only their past but also the shared journey of life that stretched endlessly before them.

That night marked a turning point; the protagonist understood more deeply the significance of traditions and storytelling in their family's life. They recognized that each story shared acted as a bridge, connecting generations while allowing the essence of love to continue dancing in the spaces left behind. Their heart full, they stepped outside into the cool night air, staring up at the stars. It felt like a promise; the little twinkling lights winking back seemed to echo the laughter and love of those who had gathered together, witness to the beauty of life's tapestry woven from shared stories. And in that quiet darkness, they realized that although loss would be a thread in their identity, it would never take the place of the love that bound them all together. The whispers of their loved one would always remain alive in the stories they told and the legacy they passed on, cascading through time like rippling waves in the vast ocean of existence.

Transforming Grief into Celebration

The evening sun dipped low on the horizon, casting a warm golden glow across the living room where the family had gathered. There was an air of quiet anticipation, the kind that hangs limply in the space between sorrow and remembrance, waiting to be filled with familiar stories and rekindled connections. The aroma of home-cooked meals wafted through the open window, mingling with the soft laughter and deep sighs of everyone present. The atmosphere was a tapestry of emotions, each thread woven with the heaviness of loss yet intertwined with the vibrant hues of shared love.

Amidst this poignant gathering, the protagonist felt an undeniable pull toward the corner of the room where a long-held family tradition awaited rejuvenation. The space bore the weight of memories each family member's absence keenly felt, yet their spirits linger, encouraging the living to celebrate their lives rather than succumb to the shadows of grief. With a gentle nod of encouragement from nearby family members, the protagonist stepped forward, ready to ignite a tradition that had been a lifeline through storms of sadness before. It began with the altar; a modest wooden table draped in a white cloth; its corners slightly frayed yet still exuding warmth and familiarity. Surrounding it were objects that whispered tales of those who had departed a well-loved teddy bear from childhood, photographs capturing laughter and joy, a faded baseball glove left just so, a delicate piece of jewelry graced with a sense of loss but also of beauty. Each item was more than a mere object; they were vessels of love; carriers of stories suspended in time.

As the protagonist placed a small, framed picture of their beloved grandmother, who always had a twinkle in her eye and fresh cookies ready on the counter, they felt a rush of bittersweet emotions bloom within. It was as if that simple act transformed the hollow ache in their chest into a soft, glowing warmth a reminder of every love-laden moment spent with her. The image captured the spirit of a woman who not only lived but who thrived in creating relationships that bled joy into every corner of their family's history. The others followed suit, bringing their own carefully chosen items, memories that encapsulated lives well-lived. A cousin placed a delicate hand-painted vase that had been their mother's, a symbol of creativity blooming within her vibrant presence.

Another family member added a fishing lure tied to the memories of days spent by the lake with an uncle who had a knack for turning every outing into an adventure. As they gathered around the memory altar, the protagonist could feel a shift within the space, a collective willingness to turn grief into celebration. The room, once heavy with the weight of sorrow, began to vibrate with an energy that felt almost tangible, a mixture of remembrance and joy, interwoven beautifully.

Each object sparked conversations, igniting shared laughter as stories unfolded in the flickering candlelight nearby where once there had been silence, there now emerged narratives bridging the gap between past and present.

"Remember the time Grandma tried to bake us a cake?" a family member chuckled, prompting a chorus of nods and laughter. "The one that turned into a gelatinous mess but still managed to taste incredible?"

The smiles erupted like fireworks, illuminating faces as the beauty of remembrance began to overshadow heartache. Within the sanctuary of the moment, the protagonist realized that in recounting those anecdotes, the characters of their deceased loved ones came alive once more, infused with the vibrancy they carried while living. With each passing story, the memory altar became a canvas painted with vivid colors, feelings spilling forth like an artist's palette. Each object instigated a wave of nostalgia; a treasure chest not only filled with sorrow but also brimming with love. There were tears, yes, but they were mingled with laughter, and the poignant contradictions created a rare kind of catharsis.

As stories wove together the past with the present, the family emerged enveloped in an emotional embrace, discovering that celebrations could culminate in both heartache and joy. Together, they lit candles one for each loved one represented. The flickering flames danced gently, casting shadows on their faces yet illuminating the room with warmth. As a family tradition took flight, the protagonist felt a profound shift grief had transported into celebration. The act of gathering to remember transformed the heavy burden of loss into a shared aura of resilience, a testament to the love that outlasts even the most profound absences. Here, in this sacred space adorned with memories, the protagonist recognized the necessity of rituals not merely as mechanisms for remembrance, but as expressions of love that could heal wounds worn down by time. Each candle served as a beacon guiding the family through despair, lighting a path composed of radiant beams of hope.

They whispered promises of continuity, transcending the fog of grief that had clouded their hearts. The protagonist crouched slightly to observe the colorful altar more closely the vibrant flowers mixed with candlelight created a palette of emotion continually shifting and evolving in its scope. Each item had a unique texture; a specific story etched into its being. The altar became a tribute to a vibrant reflection of lives well-lived, igniting flickers of joy against the backdrop of loss.

As stories continued to flow, the protagonist felt overwhelmed by the collective embrace of love that encircled them. Through active engagement with grief turning pain into celebration they witnessed the resilience that lay at the dormant edges of sorrow, waiting to be unburdened through shared remembrance. A palpable warmth enveloped the space, converting solitude into communion. In the breathing of shared narratives, pain surrendered its grip, and hope emerged as a radiant force born anew. The evening progressed, embracing a constellation of memories that entwined everyone present. They shared not only stories of lives once lived but also tales of the ways in which their loved ones had influenced the present, instilling values, love, and the courage to be themselves.

This engaged act of celebration manifested as a renewal of bonds that transcended even death. Songs of remembrance gradually filled the air the family's voices lifted together, creating harmonies reminiscent of every birthday celebration, every holiday gathering, the powerful echoes of a past where love thrived in unison. Faded melodies suddenly burst back into vivid color, revitalizing spirits worn down over time. They sang of love, life, laughter, and even moments of misunderstandings, which in retrospect whispered teachings of acceptance. It was during these moments that the protagonist realized the lesson lingering at the heart of the ritual: that grief need not solely mirror sorrow, nor should it define their memories. Instead, engaged ritualistic remembrance could birth a celebration much like the phoenix rising from its own ashes, allowing for rediscovery in shared identities rooted in love. In a world mired with loss, the protagonist understood that the necessity of this tradition wasn't simply for the deceased but also for the living. It was an antidote to isolation and a direct response to grief's often-surreal nature, transforming the experience into something tangible. Here, the alchemy of remembrance became a celebration an opportunity to affirm both the presence of loss and overwhelming gratitude for the time shared.

As the night drew to a close, the protagonist felt a sense of wholeness emerging from the fragmented pieces of their heart. The altar, a stunning homage assembled with love, radiated warmth that glimmered against the dark. Each item spoke volumes a testament to transformation as rituals turned solitude into community, engaging the living in soulful connection with those they had lost. While the tears still flowed, they were no longer solely tears of grief; now, they intermingled with the vivid colors of celebration and hope.

The protagonist understood that they would be returning to this tradition time and again, for through it lay strength, a constant reminder that love remains immortal, leaping from memory to celebration effortlessly. The memory altar now stood prominent, filled with stories, laughter, and love, a reminder that for every moment imbued with grief, there existed the promise of celebration.

Within this intricate dance between remembrance and joy, the family had discovered a path toward unity, resilience, and ultimately healing. The legacy of their loved ones would continue to bloom like the vivid flowers resting upon the altar, blossoming forth from the soil of shared memories, watering the roots of each family member intertwined in this profound human experience called life.

As they bid farewell to the evening, a sense of peace settled in, illuminating the understanding that the act of celebrating life in all its forms remains the most profound gift they could offer to those who had shaped their journey. The promise remained: to return each year, to revisit this ritual, to gather again, infusing life into memories that would continue to echo through the hallways of time reminders, not just of loss, but also of love that never fades. Each family gathered saw the stunning power of transformation, how grief intertwines with celebration, revealing the threads of hope that connect the living with those who have passed. Thus, they fostered resilience not only in their hearts but also in the collective memory shared among them, fueling the promise of enduring love.

A Garden of Fragile Wishes

Finding Sanctuary in Nature

The sun filtered softly through the canopy of ancient trees as the protagonist approached a wrought-iron gate, half hidden by overgrown ivy. It felt like a whisper from the past, a faint echo of what once thrived here. The air brimmed with a heady mixture of damp earth and blooming flowers, inviting yet laden with the weight of memory. As they pushed the gate open, its rusty hinges creaked, a sound that resonated with the very essence of hidden secrets waiting to be revealed.

Stepping through, the protagonist felt an immediate shift in atmosphere. The world beyond the gate, filled with the chaos of daily life, dwindled, replaced by a serene stillness disturbed only by the gentle rustling of leaves. Ahead lay a garden, unkempt yet captivating, as if time had surrendered its relentless grip to the tender embrace of nature.

At first, hesitation swept over them like a summer storm. Each step felt heavy, weighted down by the landscape of loss that had become too familiar. Memories of loved ones echoed in the corridors of their mind; each one a fragment of sorrow entwined with beauty. The reluctance to enter this space stemmed not just from grief, but from fear that the garden would be a reminder of what was gone, instead of a sanctuary for what could still be nurtured.

But with the first tentative step onto the soft carpet of moss, something shifted within. The protagonist noticed how the garden had its own story, a narrative woven through its wildness. Vivid splashes of color erupted all around: roses caught in moments of passionate bloom, violets peeking shyly amidst the foliage, and marigolds shouting their defiance against the muted backdrop of decay. Nature was resolute in its expression, celebrating life even as it faced the inevitability of death.

Emboldened by the vibrancy surrounding them, the protagonist took a deep breath, allowing the scents of the garden to wash over them sweet, floral fragrances mingling with the damp, earthen smell of freshly turned soil. This intoxicating blend stirred something within, beckoning them deeper into the heart of the garden, where memories could flourish, nurtured by the resilience of nature itself.

Each plant bore witness to the passage of time, standing sentinel over lives once lived and dreams that lingered like whispers in the wind. There were wildflowers that had bravely defied storms, their petals shining defiantly in hues of yellow under the fractured sunlight. Nearby, a gnarled tree trunk, bent but unbroken, reminded the protagonist of their own journey of the bends and breaks that shaped them into who they were now.

As they ventured further in, they found a small pond, its surface smooth as glass, reflecting the overhanging branches like memories reflecting back in their mind. They crouched beside it, entranced by the way the water seemed to cradle the sky, a soft reminder of the beauty that existed even in stillness. It was here that the protagonist could feel the tension within them starting to unravel, each breath seeped with tranquility.

Perhaps this garden, a hallowed sanctuary, was not merely a space to mourn, but a place to remember and create new connections. In their reflection, an image arose a loved one, long departed, dancing in a field of wildflowers, their laughter echoing like music through the ages. With each petal that unfurled, the memories of joyous moments began to reclaim a place in their heart, mingling with the sadness of loss. The absence felt less like a void and more like an invitation to preserve, to honor, and, ultimately, to allow life to flourish amid the sorrow.

The protagonist stood, gaze drifting over the peaceful tableau of the garden. A butterfly flitted by its delicate wings painted in a kaleidoscope of colors, reminding them of the fragility of life, but also its transient beauty. The garden, with its sprawling beds of flowers and gentle sway of grasses in the breeze, spoke a silent truth: that even within the realm of decay, life persisted in myriad forms. Like the cycle of the seasons, there was a promise in every blossom, a promise of renewal, of rebirth.

Encouraged by this understanding, the protagonist sank to their knees in the cool earth. Digging fingers into the soil, they embraced the tactile connection to life itself. Here, they were not just a visitor but a participant in this perennial cycle. Thoughts began to mingle with the essence of the garden, interweaving their memories with the legacy of those who had passed. Each swallowed breath carried the scent of possibility.

As they began to plant seeds in the prepared earth, they thought of the loved ones they had lost. Each seed symbolized a story, a shared smile, and the moments that made life richer. Would they bloom and flourish as a testament to the strength of love? Would they thrive amidst the chaos of life, just as the flowers standing around them? With quiet determination, they poured their hopes and memories into the soil.

The act of planting transformed each handful of earth into a sacred offering, an embodiment of promises made, and love shared. The ground, though weary and weathered, cradled each seed with care, echoing the nurturing hands that had tended to life before. In that moment, the protagonist felt connected not just to their lost loved ones but to every soul that had ever sought refuge in nature's embrace.

The sun arced higher in the sky, illuminating the intricacies of the garden with brilliant light. Shadows danced, and the air buzzed with the soft hum of life still thriving in its myriad forms. The protagonist looked around, absorbing the vivid tableau, a fervent reminder that beauty existed even beyond hardship. Time slipped effortlessly away, and as the protagonist continued to plant seeds, they realized that they were also tending to their own heart.

With every memory unearthed and every hope expressed through the dirt, they discovered resilience in vulnerability. This garden had become a sanctuary not a reminder of what was, but a promise of what could still be cultivated. Their fingers stained with earth, the protagonist sat back on their heels, taking in the transformation of their emotional landscape alongside the garden's own rebirth.

This hidden haven had revealed its truth, not as a reminder of decay, but as proof of life's cyclical nature where every end gave rise to new beginnings. In this sacred space, the protagonist slowly allowed themselves to embrace both the light and the shadows of their journey. They recognized that to fully honor their losses, one needed to acknowledge the pain and allow it to mingle with the joyful recollections.

The act of nurturing this garden of memories would not only fortify their connection to loved ones long gone but also create room for new life, new dreams, new loves to emerge in the future. As the sun began to sink in the sky, casting warm golden hues across the landscape, the protagonist felt a sense of peace enveloping them. A clarity took shape in their mind.

This garden wasn't merely a surface of soil and plants, it was a metaphorical space where memories could flourish amidst growth and decay, a refuge where they could return again and again to nourish the threads of love. They walked back towards the wrought-iron gate, taking care to close it gently behind them. With each step, they turned their thoughts to the seeds nestled in the earth, imagining how they would thrive as seasons changed.

They felt a renewed sense of purpose, a quiet assurance that loss did not equate to an end, but rather, stirred an invitation to new beginnings. As they left the garden behind, the protagonist turned to glance one last time at the vibrant array of colors peeking through the foliage. They vowed to return, not just as an act of remembrance, but as a meaningful ritual woven into their narrative of life commitment to ensure that love and memory would always coalesce within the sanctuary of nature's embrace.

The hidden garden returned to its stillness, maintaining its secrets and stories. It thrived not only on the remnants of pain but also on remembrance and the act of nurturing an eternal dance reflecting the essence of humanity's journey through love, loss, and everything in between.

Planting Seeds of Remembrance

As the sun crested the horizon, its light began to filter through the canopy of branches overhead, casting patches of warm golden hues onto the ground. The garden was awakening, each petal unfurling with an eager anticipation, as if joining in on the protagonist's journey of remembrance. It was a new day, a blank canvas awaiting the strokes of memory, and the protagonist stood at the threshold, shovel in hand, ready to dig deep into the rich soil of their past.

With each thrust of the spade, they unearthed the earth, creating little homes for the seeds that they would plant seeds not just of flowers, but of stories, of laughter, and of love. Each seed held the essence of a cherished moment or a lesson learned at the hands of those who had left an indelible mark on their life. As they knelt, the cool dampness of the soil beneath their fingers felt like a tangible connection to those memories, grounding them in the present while drawing on the past.

The first seed was small, almost unassuming, but within it lay the vibrant hues of a summer day spent with Grandma Helen in her backyard. The protagonist recalled how they would race to the old oak tree, her laughter ringing clear as they rolled down the hillside, the smell of freshly cut grass lingering in the air. They glanced up at the towering oak, its strong branches spreading out like a protective embrace. Grandma had often shared stories under that tree, tales woven with wisdom and affection. As they placed the seed into its new home, a soft whisper echoed across the garden, a reminder of the lessons of patience and resilience.

Watering the seed, they mused that nurturing an idea requires just as much care and attention as nurturing a plant. Grandma always said, "What you tend to will flourish."

Next came the seed that held the essence of the bond with their brother, Jamie. Memories collided as they remembered nights filled with shared secrets and laughter, the way Jamie's mischievous smile could brighten even the darkest of days. They envisioned their late-night adventures, sneaking cookies from the jar at midnight, whispering silly stories about monsters they both imagined lurking under the bed. This seed would symbolize the joy of camaraderie of shared dreams they had dared to dream big together.

As they watered this seed, their heartfelt tears mingled with the soil, enriching it and sending down a prayer whispered with each droplet: "Let joy find its way into our lives again."

With every new seed, the protagonist narrated more stories aloud, tales of courage, heartbreak, triumph, and loss. They spoke about Aunt Mae, who taught them not just how to bake, but how to embrace life with an open heart. Each time they stirred the batter, they could hear her encouraging words echoing in their mind like a comforting lullaby:

"Life is sweet, even when it's bittersweet."

The seed representing this memory seemed larger, almost heavy with the weight of all that Aunt Mae had shared. Watering it, the protagonist realized that recalling these stories was both a tribute and a denial of death; it was a way to keep alive the spirit of those who had formed the fabric of their being.

In that moment, surrounded by soft rustling leaves and the gentle hum of nature, it became increasingly clear that this act of planting was not merely about growing a garden. It was about reconnecting with the abundance of memories buried deep within about cultivating resilience as they faced the fragility of life. How easy it could be to overlook such beauty amidst the turmoil of grief! But each memory planted was a hope, an invitation to grow something beautiful, something that could blossom despite, or even because of, the pain of loss.

The garden was becoming a mural of remembrance, each section dedicated to different aspects of love lost. As they worked, they thought about nurturing this garden the way they needed to tend to their own heart and mind. The journey of fostering memories was collective; it transcended the individual experience and spoke to the universal truths of human connection.

With each seed planted, they sparked the act of remembrance, knowing that others could partake in this legacy. It was their way of inviting joy back into life amidst sorrow of fostering new beginnings that felt impossibly distant just days ago.

As they turned to the next seed, the one to honor their father, waves of nostalgia washed over them. Memories surged forth of weekends spent fishing by the lake, of patient storytelling while waiting for the fish to bite. Those afternoons had felt timeless, filled with laughter, lessons, and the slow, comforting rhythm of life. They could still hear their father's voice cutting through the gentle lapping of water, explaining the delicate balance of nature intertwined with family.

Placing this seed carefully into the earth, they breathed in the rich, earthy scent, whispering, "Each lesson will grow, just like the love you gave."

With every story shared, as they nourished the seeds, they began to notice something magical happening in the garden. Bumps began to rise from the soil where they had planted; tender shoots of green with the promise of life began to push through. It was as if the garden itself echoed the protagonist's heart, responding in kind to every sigh of remembrance and every drop of grief that watered the earth.

This slow emergence mirrored their journey from the depths of sorrow; hope was beginning to sprout. Days turned into weeks, and as they tended the garden, the flowers gradually bloomed, releasing fragrances that mingled in the air, heartfelt reminders of love that transcended mortal bounds. Each blossoming flower was a testament to the memories that had taken root, a validation of stories that deserved to be shared.

The protagonist could feel the energy shift; the heaviness of grief slowly being tempered by the vibrant colors of remembrance. Each flower in the garden became a narrative, a nod to the lives lived, each hue capturing the complexity of joy and sorrow. The soft lavender represented Grandma Helen, while the bright yellow blooms sang of Jamie's playful spirit. There were white daisies for Aunt Mae, signifying the sweetness of life, and deep crimson roses honoring the love shared with their father.

Visitors began to wander in and out of the garden, drawn to its beauty, and the protagonist welcomed them with open arms. Friends and family would stop by to share their stories, each adding another layer to the tapestry of remembrance. They began to recognize the shared nature of grief, the notion that no one is alone in their losses, that community bonds are fortified through collective memory.

The garden transformed into a sanctuary, a sacred place where conversations flowed freely among blooming flowers, and laughter mingled with tears. And so, it became a place where people would gather, sharing not just their own experiences of grief but also how they, too, kept memories alive and cultivated grace within their sorrow.

Stories emerged not like burdens but as shared truths, affirming life even in the face of death. The protagonist realized that through active engagement with memories, they were not only cultivating flowers but nurturing connections both with those who had passed and those still living. Each story planted a new seed, expanding the garden beyond its initial confines.

Seasons turned in their garden, and with time, the protagonist witnessed the maturation of not just the flowers, but their understanding of loss. They began incorporating rituals into their routine, lighting candles on the anniversaries of their loved ones, gathering friends to share stories, to reminisce, and to celebrate. The garden had become a living library of shared experiences, an open invitation to anyone searching for solace amidst loss.

Through this journey, the protagonist discovered that grief, while deeply isolating, could paradoxically bring people together, stitching the fabric of communal identity through shared reminiscence. Their initial hesitance morphed into a sense of duty to foster a space where remembrance could flourish openly, unbridled by the shadows of sorrow.

And in these moments of remembrance, they finally understood that planting seeds of remembrance wasn't merely an act of paying tribute to the past, it was a proactive embrace of life itself. It was recognizing that while the ghosts of loss would always be present, so too would the lessons learned, the love shared, the laughter exchanged, and the memories kept alive through time.

With each passing day, the garden continued to beckon new

visitors, embracing the ebb and flow of life and death. The act of remembrance became a woven tapestry of healing, where each thread shone with the unique essence of every life touched. The protagonist found themselves inextricably linked to all those who wandered their path, all of whom imparted stories that served as powerful reminders of resilience, connection, and grace in the face of inevitable sorrow.

In return, the flowers blossomed with an urgency to remind the protagonist and their visitors that not only did memories reside in the past, but they also held the power to shape the present and beckon a hopeful future. The delicate balance between joy and grief continued to intertwine, a reminder that every moment, whether of happiness or sorrow, was part of a larger narrative woven with love, connecting yearning hearts who had once roamed this earth, leaving their indelible marks behind like vibrant colors stretched upon the canvas of existence.

What had once begun as an attempt to simply tend a garden transformed into an exploration of human experience, showing that active engagement with memory could cultivate an everlasting legacy of love and hope.

In this garden of fragile wishes, every seed planted, and every story shared became a guidepost along the way a sanctuary thriving against the seasonal winds of change, a symbol that love transcends the boundaries of time and space, flourishing even in the delicate place where grief meets remembrance.

The Blooms of Resilience

The morning light cast a gentle glow over the garden, illuminating the dewdrops clinging to the petals of flowers that bowed under the weight of their own beauty. The protagonist, overwhelmed yet determined, knelt amidst a sea of vibrant colors, evidence of both the fragility and resilience of life. Each bloom beckoned as an embodiment of memories cherished and emotions layered deeply beneath the surface, urging the protagonist to delve into the complex tapestry of their own grief and recovery.

With every hand that brushed against the soft petals, the protagonist felt a stirring within, a bubbling connection to warmth and sorrow alike, two intertwined threads that together formed the fabric of their existence. This garden, with its fragrant bursts of lilac and powerful sunflowers, had become a sanctuary, a sacred ground where they could confront unexpressed emotions and acknowledge the beauty found within pain.

The act of nurturing the garden felt like a ritual, a re-commitment to the process of healing that had begun in dark corners of their heart. As the protagonist dug their fingers into the soil, they planted the seeds not just of flowers, but of hope, the kind of hope rooted in shared experiences, laughter, and the lessons their loved ones had imparted before leaving this world.

They recalled moments spent under the open sky, gathering with loved ones, laughter ringing out like the sweetest melody. The memory felt alive in the moment, seemingly sprouting from the very earth they tended to. Time slipped away as they toiled, sweat beading on their brow, a reminder that growth requires effort and patience. They thought of the cycle of life, a circle that encapsulated beginnings, endings, and new beginnings again.

With that thought, they instinctively reached out towards the vibrant blooms surrounding them, feeling as if each one mirrored a moment of love or loss from their life. They paused to reflect on the significance of the garden and the act of remembrance.

"How strange it is to know that beauty so profound can sprout from the ashes of sorrow," they murmured to themselves, their voice mingling with the buzzing of nearby bees. In that quiet moment, they recognized the profound truth that their journey through grief was laden with hidden potential for healing.

Those flowers, each unique in shape, color, and fragrance, embodied various emotions. From the delicate white daisies signaling innocence and remembrance to the rich crimson blooms that exuded passions long past, each petal bore a story worth telling. The protagonist gathered small handfuls of soil, sifting it gently through their fingers before letting it fall back to the earth, much like how memories surface and sink within our consciousness.

They began to long for a deeper understanding of how to cultivate not only the garden but also their own spirit. As they tended to the blossoms, flowers began to emerge that symbolized resilience, hardy marigolds that thrived even amidst the harshest conditions, and delicate orchids that whispered tales of survival against the odds.

They envisioned the marigolds as bold reminders of challenges faced and complexities embraced, each bud a reflection of the journey they had been navigating since loss had entered their life. The task at hand became deeply meditative the rhythmic action of watering, pruning, and caring infused them with a sense of purpose and connection.

They allowed their mind to wander, contemplating the interplay between sorrow and joy, how each emotion added depth to their flourishing landscape. Emerging from this contemplation was a newfound appreciation for the disparate feelings lodged in their heart. With each passing day, the protagonist embraced this metaphorical garden as a realm for exploration and discovery.

The way the flowers welcomed the light warmed their heart. Resilience blossomed all around them, and they took solace in the knowledge that their emotional landscape mirrored that of the garden, though it weathered storms and bouts of despair, life continued to flourish in unexpected ways.

They began to harvest blossoms of joy from memories, cradling each delicate stem in their hands. It was a breathtaking process, reminiscent of gathering rich stories woven over years, stories that ebbed and flowed like the seasons, adapting but never disappearing for good.

This ritual of harvesting became a tangible representation of how joy can spring forth from the most painful places. It was this very act that opened a floodgate, allowing them to recognize how intertwined love and grief truly are, revealing the pathways toward deeper understanding and acceptance.

On a particularly bright afternoon, as they meandered through the flourishing landscape, the protagonist paused at a cluster of sunflowers, the kind that always stretched vigorously towards the sun. They couldn't help but smile, realizing that sunflowers mirrored their own journey towards light, reflecting an innate desire to embrace joy even in the face of shadows.

Each sunflower stood tall, bold, and unapologetic, a living symbol of the courage churning within their spirit. It suddenly struck them: "Each blossom celebrates not just the individual it represents, but also the vibrant legacy of connections that endure beyond the confines of this life."

In this moment, inspiration flowed like a river through their veins, igniting an impulse to gather others into the garden, a place where both joy and sorrow could coexist. They envisioned creating gatherings amidst the blooms, encouraging others to share their own stories of love, loss, and resilience, a place for remembrance and healing, weaving together the narratives of loved ones into the fabric of the flowers, washed in the warm golden hues of the setting sun.

They marveled at the thought of how vulnerability inevitably leads to connection. This realization washed over them like a gentle breeze that rustled through the leaves, energizing their spirit and compelling them to take action.

They envisioned a community gathering of souls within the sanctuary of the garden, a collective of stories signaling hope amidst grief and celebrating the enduring power of love. In the days that followed, they invited friends, family, and even neighbors to join them in the garden, and slowly but surely, it transformed into a vibrant tapestry of shared experiences.

People brought items that evoked cherished memories stones painted with inspiring messages, photographs that depicted moments of joy, and handwritten letters left beneath the blooms, whispering memories for the wind to carry. The first gathering pulsated with nostalgia and warmth. The air was fragrant with the scent of flowers and robust laughter.

It was a safe haven, where everyone found comfort in the company of one another, crafting a newfound understanding of their emotional landscapes. Sharing stories became a sacred testament to the resilience each person embodied the laughter, tears, and shared memories creating a symphony of interconnected lives.

On that day, it dawned upon them just how powerful collective remembrance can be. They bore witness to the healing effects of community as they sat among friends, fortified by the garden's embrace. They saw how emotions poured forth freely, stories woven from shared experiences in which joy intertwined with sorrow, each voice contributing its unique melody to the overarching harmony.

As laughter erupted amidst poignant tales, the protagonist felt an overwhelming sense of belonging, an affirmation that love never truly disappears itself into the very roots that feed the flowers, charging every petal with meaning and connection.

It was a moment of euphoria as they kneeled among their friends, hands dirty from planting seeds together, marveling at how each shared story created blooms of resilience nurtured by love. In the days that followed, the protagonist observed how the garden began to thrive not only because of their actions but because of the love and memories infused by others who participated in nurturing it.

The garden flourished, symbolizing not only the beauty of life but also the strength in accepting the intertwined relationship between love and loss. As time passed, the protagonist collected blossoms and arranged them into bouquets to take home as blessed reminders. Each bouquet represented a unique story, capturing raw moments that intertwined lives had shared, echoing laughter amid sorrow, a bittersweet tableau that revealed the complexity of human emotions.

They often returned to the garden, finding solace in the blooms that waved gently in the breeze, holding space for their thoughts and feelings. The blooms of resilience transformed into a ritual of sorts as the seasons turned. Spring banners with bursts of color became symbols of renewal, a reminder that rebirth intertwined with loss allows us to embrace life more fully.

Warm summer days followed, vibrant colors catching the sunlight, and the protagonist often found themselves reminiscing on distinct moments. A tender smile crept upon their lips, illuminated by the knowledge that positivity could plant itself in the broken remnants of sorrow. It was here that they learned beauty often rises through cracks,perseverance that breaks through the surface toward the light.

Autumn embraced the garden as the leaves began to fall, echoing another cycle in the dance of life and change. The protagonist leaned closer to trace their fingers along the edges of fading blooms, recognizing the beauty in their impermanence. In this very act, they found solace, becoming acquainted with the natural ebb and flow of life and love, a reminder that just as one season may yield to another, so too can grief transform into acceptance.

During these quiet autumn evenings, as the sun dipped low behind the horizon, casting warm hues across the garden, the protagonist often engaged in conversations with the spirits of those they had lost. It was here, as the stars erupted into view, that they settled upon the rich notion that memories had an eternal core that extends far beyond mortal longing.

The blooms of resilience thrived under both sun and shadow, unfurling their colors like stories told in the whispers of loved ones long gone. The protagonist planted those memories into their heart, nourishing them like seeds that would tell tales of joy and contribute to the ongoing legacy of love.

They recognized that a garden won't stay untouched it evolves, embodies, and acknowledges the seasons of life. It was in this continuous cycle that they found power, a newfound appreciation for the dynamic flow of human emotion, a collage of both loss and laughter, light and dark.

The garden became a metaphor not just for healing but as a reminder that continuity was woven through every moment, every story shared. With each passing season, the protagonist celebrated the blooms that took root and thrived, reminders of experiences to embrace. They often expressed gratitude for the old leaves that fell, making way for new life, a tangible metaphor for the beauty embedded in every goodbye, signaling a hopeful promise of what would come next.

From this intimacy developed a profound understanding of how one could easily collapse beneath the weight of loss, but nurtured by the soil of shared history, sorrow gracefully transforms into beauty. As they explored these emotional depths, they found the garden was more than just a patch of earth, it was fundamentally an arrangement of their own heart, blooming anew despite wear and tear.

From the richness of their realization emerged a new legacy, the understanding that nurturing both the garden and oneself produces blooms of resilience that extends into perpetuity, rippling through time as living testaments of love and loss. Not only for the departed but in honor of future generations nurtured by remembrance and shared bonds, rooted deeply into the fabric of humanity.

As seasons shifted and time stretched forth, the protagonist transformed their journey through growth and grief into a legacy through which others could find healing. They advocated for gathering again each time amid the vibrant colors of the garden united in both love and sorrow, sharing the stories of those who had come before, sowing seeds of hope that would flower into remembrance.

So, the garden stood a sanctuary thrumming with life. A place where blooms of resilience flourished under the watchful eye of love, and where human hearts became unbreakable when they learned to nurture each other amidst their delicate fragility. It became a tapestry spun of joy, heartache, and interconnectedness that openly welcomed everyone to wander through the garden of fragile wishes, allowing them to reclaim the beauty that thrives even amid the complexities of existence.

As the protagonist stood in the garden's embrace, they smiled fondly, acknowledging that each bloom spoke a language of its own. The vibrant colors mirrored the multifaceted experiences of life; the bittersweet, intertwined threads of resilience and vulnerability danced in the golden rays of sunlight.

In the gentle rustle of leaves above, the chorus of unseen spirits sang, telling tales of love, loss, and the enduring strength of the human spirit. And the protagonist felt the whispers of those who had touched their life, guiding them, reminding them that their hearts were forever entwined with the vibrant blooms of resilience, flourishing even in the shadows.

The Void of
Unlived Life

Confronting the Unfulfilled

The first rays of dawn peeked through the window as the protagonist sat on the edge of their bed, staring blankly at the wall opposite. It was a familiar place, yet today it felt different weighted with a heaviness that seemed to seep into the very fabric of the morning. They could hear the soft chirping of birds and the distant sound of a lawnmower starting up somewhere down the street. Life continued beyond these four walls, but within this room, time had stalled the moment they received the news, the moment they learned that their loved one had been taken too soon.

What dreams had slipped through the cracks of existence with them? The protagonist's mind drifted into a murky fog of memories, stirring images of shared aspirations that had flickered like candle flames bright yet fragile, poised to extinguish at any moment. Here, amid the sorrow, lay a turbulent sea of unfulfilled potential. Each wave crashing against the shores of their consciousness carried a reminder of everything that would now remain forever unspoken, unseen, and undone.

Their loved one had often spoken of traveling the world of walking the ancient ruins of Rome, tasting the spices of Morocco, and dancing joyfully on the vibrant streets of Rio de Janeiro. Each plan, wrapped in enthusiasm, had been laced with the promise of tomorrow that now shimmered like a mirage on an endless horizon, beautiful yet utterly out of reach. With each memory that surfaced, the protagonist felt the tide of grief rising, an overwhelming mix of sadness and anger. How could the world continue turning, blissfully unaware of what had been lost?

The light crept further into the room, illuminating photographs that adorned the walls, smiling faces of happy moments frozen in time, now heavy with the weight of absence. They traced a finger over the frame of a photograph where laughter had once echoed like music. They could almost hear the joyous sound of their loved one's laughter, a melody that had now fallen silent. Panic rose within them, gripping their chest with a strength that stoked the fires of regret. What did their loved one want most? What walls had they yearned to tear down? Dreams, once tangible, now felt like gossamer threads, too delicate to grasp yet impossible to let go.

Each aspiration became a ghost haunting the edges of the protagonist's mind, shadows that spoke of a future that would never arrive. Day after day, the echo of unrealized potential is intertwined with the aching hollow in the protagonist's heart. The living world outside their window contrasted starkly with their internal landscape. Everywhere they looked, they were reminded of all the possibilities stolen. They wandered through their thoughts like a drifter lost in an endless maze, each twist revealing a new pang of disappointment, an untraveled road, a book unwritten, and a song unsung.

In the days that followed, a routine began to form, a ritual of remembrance amid the crippling sorrow. They found themselves standing in the living room, the faint scent of last night's dinner still lingering in the air. It was familiar ground; a place of warmth and laughter once filled with the vibrant energy of companionship. Yet now, it felt like an empty vessel adrift in an ocean of grief.

They began to collect and gather the items once cherished, fragments of their loved one's essence, to create a memory altar, a sacred space honoring a life lived and dreams unfulfilled. Each object told a story: a worn-out passport with scribbled notes of places they would have visited; a battered guitar that longed to strum the melodies they had sung together; photographs of countless sunsets witnessed, each moment now etched with longing.

As the protagonist arranged the altar, tears streamed down their face. It was a bittersweet exercise, one that drew out the sharpness of grief but also lit soft embers of love and remembrance. They recalled the long walks through the park where conversations flowed freely, shared secrets fluttering like autumn leaves on a crisp day. These moments were treasures, yet they felt marred by the weight of what could never be.

With each day, they faced the unsettling reality that while life continued for others, the dreams of the departed had dissipated into thin air. What would their loved one think if they could see this? Would they feel sorrow for the untraveled paths or joy in the memories left behind? A voice in the protagonist's head whispered that they should have pursued the journeys, chased the ambitions, if only they had known their time would be so painfully short.

One evening, overwhelmed by a swell of emotion, they dared to write a letter to their loved one, a letter filled with all the things left unsaid. "I wish you could have seen Paris in the spring," they wrote, reminiscing about conversations that emerged like fireflies on warm summer nights. "I wonder how bright your smile would have been as we walked along the Seine, feeling the pulse of life thrumming around us."

With each line, they poured out a river of hopes dashed, both theirs and their loved ones. The words tumbled one after another on the page, raw and unfiltered. "What would you have accomplished? What dreams would you have achieved?" The protagonist grappled with the haunting nature of unresolved questions. They envisioned the countless milestones, birthdays celebrated, dreams chased, love shared, lives enriched.

Eventually, the letter became a dialogue, a way to confront the bittersweet ache that occupied their being. The act of writing became a bridge over the void, a connection to what had been irrevocably lost. As they sealed the envelope, they felt a slight weight lift, as if acknowledging their fears had rendered them less daunting, somehow more bearable.

Time passed, yet the aching sense of unfulfilled dreams never fully subsided. Instead, it transformed. The protagonist began to view it through a lens that combined love with acceptance. They set out to uncover the dreams of their loved ones, gathering insights from those who had known them best. Friends and family began to share their stories, painting a vivid portrait of unexpressed hopes and desires.

In these conversations, a complex tapestry emerged, full of colors, stories of places longed for, dreams nurtured in whispers, and passions ignited by fleeting moments. The protagonist learned that their loved one had aspirations beyond great travel and adventures; there was a desire to create, to express, to make an impact. They had wanted to write a novel, to weave their experiences into a narrative that resonated with others.

As these revelations unfolded, the protagonist felt sparks of inspiration fueling their grief. Perhaps it was time to carry forward some of the dreams left unpursued. What if they, too, began writing? It would be an homage, a labor of love, weaving together the lost threads of their loved one's potential with their own journey. They imagined filling pages with stories that held not only their memories but also those of the shared experiences that transcended the boundaries of life and death.

In an unexpected twist of fate, the protagonist found solace in creativity. It became their lifeline, a way to navigate the rough seas of sorrow while keeping the flame of their loved one's spirit alive. They poured their heart into the words, crafting narratives that danced on the edges of memory. It was as if the essence of their loved one was guiding them through the process, whispering encouragement with every keystroke.

Within the creative process, blossomed a further realization. No longer was their grief simply a burden weighing them down; it began to transform into a powerful catalyst for expression, a channel through which love flowed freely. As they explored their loved one's unfulfilled dreams, breathing life into the stories left untold, it became clear that honoring those dreams did not merely reside in mourning but in the resolute act of living forward.

Even in the shadow of loss, the protagonist unearthed the beauty of unfulfilled ambitions. They discovered that dreams don't vanish, they simply evolve. The act of confronting those dreams added depth to their understanding of what it means to truly live. No longer were they shackled by regret; instead, they learned to dance with grief and hope.

Over time, the memory altar evolved, blossoming into a creative sanctuary. Pages filled with stories adorned the walls, each piece resonating with the essence of their loved one. They felt their presence in every word, a comforting reminder of dreams and aspirations that continued to linger in the folds of their heart.

As the protagonist gazed upon the altar one evening,

illuminated by the soft glow of candles flickering in gentle rhythm, they experienced an epiphany. The void left by their loved one could never be entirely filled, but in giving voice to dreams unfulfilled, they discovered a way to weave these silken threads into the fabric of their existence.

Love, after all, transcended even the boundaries of life, woven into the stories shared, the memories echoed, and the aspirations fulfilled. In that breath of quiet determination, the protagonist lifted the pen once more, ready to write not just for themselves but for their loved one, a tribute to dreams, love, and the boundless resilience of spirit.

It was here, in honoring the unfulfilled, that they finally found reconciliation, walking hand in hand with the echoes of what once was, embracing the unfolding journey of what could still be.

Embracing the Courage to Live

The morning sun streamed through the thin curtains of the protagonist's bedroom, casting a warm glow that felt both inviting and alien. The remnants of grief lingered in every corner, yet the promise of a new day stirred something deep within, a longing for purpose, a spark of courage to reclaim life. It was time to move beyond the suffocating embrace of loss and confront the potential that lay unclaimed in the depths of the void.

With a heavy heart, but a spirit yearning for liberation, the protagonist pulled on a comfortable pair of shoes and ventured outdoors. Each step felt akin to shedding layers of sorrow, replaced with a tentative hope. The air was crisp, and the world teemed with life; birds chirped in the trees, and the gentle rustle of leaves in the wind seemed to whisper encouragement. It was as if nature itself conspired to remind the protagonist that life continues even in the wake of loss.

As they navigated through the neighborhood, memories battled for attention, fragments of laughter shared with the departed floated like colorful butterflies in the mind. The protagonist hesitated for a moment, haunted by the thought of how the pain of absence often shackled these memories. But today, there was a subtle shift; today, they decided to honor those memories by allowing them to breathe freely, as one would release a captive bird.

Their footfalls brought them to a small café that held significance from happier times. The scent of freshly brewed coffee wafted through the air, coaxing the protagonist inside. It was a cozy place, filled with the comforting sounds of conversations, laughter, and clinking cups. There, at a familiar corner table, sat Anna, an old friend who had been a silent pillar throughout the ordeal.

"Hey! You made it," Anna beamed, her enthusiasm radiating warmth that enveloped the protagonist.

"I'm trying," was the tentative response, but the faint hint of a smile tugged at the corners of their lips.

"Good! Celebrating small victories today, remember?" Anna encouraged, sliding a cup of steaming coffee across the table.

"Right, small victories," they echoed, taking a sip and savoring the moment.

Anna leaned closer, her eyes reflecting a depth of understanding. "You know, it's okay to feel everything you're feeling. But have you thought about what it might mean to celebrate the lives that were?"

The question struck a chord, resonating deep within.

"I've been thinking about that a lot lately. It feels wrong to move on, doesn't it?" The protagonist's voice wavered, caught between the weight of grief and the lightening potential of acceptance.

"Moving on doesn't mean forgetting. It means integrating those memories into who you are now. It's about celebrating your life, too," Anna replied, her voice calm yet insistent. "Living authentically is the greatest tribute you can give them. It honors their memory while allowing you to embrace your own aspirations."

A flicker of hope ignited in the protagonist. Could this be true? The idea of using their experiences to fuel the pursuit of life felt both exhilarating and terrifying.

"What if I fail? What if I can't fill the void?"

Anna placed a reassuring hand over theirs. "What if you soar? What if you discover new depths of joy, love, and fulfillment? Every time you embrace those feelings, you honor them. You're already so much more than your grief."

The conversation shifted as they delved into shared memories, each story a thread woven into the fabric of their collective experience. Laughter erupted over anecdotes of mischief, love, and mistakes, and with each chuckle, the weight of loss lifted just a little.

"Remember that time we got lost on that hiking trail?" Anna's eyes sparkled, her smile infectious.

"How could I forget? We ended up in that tiny diner miles from where we started," the protagonist responded, a genuine smile breaking free.

"You were so determined to find your way back! That stubbornness got us into so much trouble."

"And yet, it brought adventure," they sighed, realization echoing loudly.

Those moments were just as significant as the painful ones. They encapsulated life's unpredictability, its beauty, and the shared journey of those who mattered.

After their coffee was finished, the protagonist felt invigorated with a new sense of clarity. As they walked with Anna back toward the park, they found themselves lost in thought, how often had they relegated joy to the shadows, fearing it would offend the memory of their loved ones? But what if embracing that joy brought them closer to understanding love's permanence?

"Let's walk for a bit," Anna suggested as they reached the park. "The air will help clear your mind."

Strolling through the park, they observed families, couples, and friends engrossed in their own stories. The laughter of children echoed in the background, reminding them of spontaneous moments of joy that could erupt anywhere.

"People look so happy," the protagonist mused.

"It's contagious, isn't it?" Anna smiled, glancing at a group picnicking nearby. "What if we joined them?"

Without fully understanding the impulse, the protagonist felt a surge of courage, a chance beckoning them to step outside the safety of reserved grief.

Anna raised an eyebrow teasingly. "I like the way you think! Let's go spread some cheer."

Propelled by newfound determination, they approached the carefree group, laughter spilling from their lips as they exchanged pleasantries. Introductions were made, stories exchanged, and the protagonist realized how easy it was to connect with others when they let down their walls. Each friendly interaction was nourishing, a reminder that love thrived in shared experiences.

As the day melted into evening, they found themselves surrounded by people they had only just met. Upbeat conversation flowed effortlessly, laughter merging with the sounds of the park. It was in this light-hearted camaraderie that the protagonist truly began to grasp the essence of resilience.

They watched as people shared their own burdens, losses, disappointments, and dreams deferred, yet the stories were underscored with encouragement and hope. They were no longer solo travelers in their wandering grief; rather, they were amid a vast community that carried its own scars yet radiated strength.

One woman, an artist named Clara, shared how she had found inspiration in her late mother's favorite songs. "I paint to honor her memory," Clara explained. "Each stroke carries forward the love we shared, the lessons she imparted. She may be gone, but her essence lives on through my work."

The conversation turned to the theme of embracing dreams, and the protagonist pondered Clara's assertion. How had they allowed grief to dictate their aspirations? The fear of detached life had muted their ambitions, but here was tangible proof that creativity flourished through loss. Clara's experience was a vibrant reminder that in honoring the departed, one could still live boldly.

Feeling emboldened, the protagonist took a deep breath, summoning their voice. "I've felt stuck, afraid to pursue my dreams because it felt wrong to focus on anything other than my loss. But hearing your stories is... is awakening something in me."

The collective gaze turned towards them, each face an embodiment of understanding and support.

"What is it that you've wanted to pursue?" Clara encouraged gently.

"I always wanted to write," they confessed, words tumbling out like hesitant raindrops.

"Then write!" Anna said, her voice charged with enthusiasm. "There's no better time than now. If your loved one inspired you, allow their influence to guide your pen."

"Yes! Just imagine how healing that could be," Clara added, her eyes sparking with excitement.

The conversation lifted the protagonist higher, light illuminating the corners of their heart where shadows had long dwelled. Each new voice resonated with encouragement, creating a symphony of support that nurtured an intoxicating feeling of possibility. It was exhilarating to embrace the courage to pursue a path they had once thought abandoned.

As twilight descended, one by one, warm farewells were exchanged. The protagonist departed with a renewed sense of empowerment, grateful for the resilience of the human spirit and its capacity to rise amid heartache.

In the solitude of their room later that night, the protagonist sat at their desk, heart racing in anticipation. They opened a journal that had remained unopened for weeks, its pages blank but full of potential. Cradling a pen, they took a moment and inhaled deeply, memories flooding back, and with each stroke of the pen, they began to breathe life into their narratives.

"You are worthy of this joy," the echo of Anna's voice reverberated in their mind, reminding them that every word captured was a stitch in the fabric of their existence. They wrote not only for themselves but as an act of remembrance, for those they had loved, those they had lost, and those who had shaped their journey.

Days turned into weeks as the protagonist poured their heart onto the pages. They wrote of grief, but also of laughter and joy, love shared in fleeting moments, and experiences that propelled them toward acceptance. The fear of the void lingered, but with every story written, it gradually transformed into a reservoir of strength.

Through every narrative, courageous encounters unfolded on the page, the protagonist embraced and celebrated life with renewed vigor. They explored places packed with memories, investing time in friendships that blossomed anew. With Anna's encouragement, they participated in local writing workshops, where every shared story became a bridge to understanding, accountability, and a community blossoming in creativity.

In one such workshop, they met Jeremy, a fellow writer grappling with the recent loss of his sister. Over coffee one afternoon, they shared their struggles and aspirations.

"I thought writing would help me find some closure, but I feel everything is still so jumbled," Jeremy confessed, running a hand through his hair in frustration.

"You're not alone," the protagonist reassured him. "It's all part of the process. Writing may not provide immediate answers, but it captures the nuances of our journey, helping us make sense of emotions as we navigate through them."

Jeremy nodded contemplatively. "But what if it feels too

overwhelming?"

Their spirits ignited, the protagonist replied, "Then write through the overwhelm. Let your pen dance across the page, guiding you even when the clarity feels distant. We're all in this together, sharing the burden and the light."

The camaraderie built between them created a rich tapestry of shared experiences, laughter interwoven with vulnerability. It was remarkable how journeys could intertwine, converging on themes of strength and courage, fostering growth in the depths of love.

They discovered that grief, while deep and often isolating, could serve as the catalyst for transformation and authenticity. Vulnerability began to resonate at the heart of their connection, each encounter sparking deeper introspection. They learned to balance sadness with gratitude, embracing the duality of their existence while encouraging one another to dream toward the future.

Together, they crafted stories that celebrated life in all its complexity, reclaiming dreams that had once been defined by the void.

As months rolled by, the protagonist's desire to celebrate life through writing extended beyond personal reflections. Soon, they proposed a community event, a gathering to honor lives lost and share stories of resilience and love. Their vision was to create a platform that championed joy, creativity, and courage amidst heartache.

At the event, families and friends gathered, sharing their stories with poignant grace, paint striding across canvases as artists captured the essence of love and memory. The atmosphere buzzed with empathy; music filled the air, melodies reflecting hope that vibrated from one heart to another.

As the protagonist took to the stage, nerves tingled at the base of their spine, but as they looked out into the crowd, solace found its way into their heart. A shared understanding enveloped them, those present had similarly grappled with grief's weight, yet here they stood, united in purpose.

"I invite you all to share your stories today," they began, their voice steady, filled with resolve. "To celebrate the lives that shaped us, to embrace the courage we found in their absence, and to honor the dreams that will carry us forward."

As hands raised in eager participation, the protagonist felt a deep sense of belonging wash over them, a moment stretching beyond the individual experience, merging their voices into a beautiful tapestry reflecting humanity's myriad threads.

The event glowed with laughter among tears; connection felt affirming. People spoke of loved ones, of dreams unrealized yet carried forth into the present, memories, once heavy weights, became catalysts igniting hope anew.

In that moment, the protagonist realized they had transcended the void that once threatened to drown them. They had woven their grief into a rich narrative, allowing it to coalesce into a celebration of life, launching them toward authenticity and igniting aspirations long dormant.

In time, they too stepped forward to share a story, feeling wrapped up in the warmth of shared experience.

"I stand before you today not just to remember but to embrace the courage to live. To realize that our loved ones remain present in our hearts every step we take forward. Each day is a canvas waiting for vibrant strokes of joy; each story shared is life being honored."

As they spoke, voices chimed in with knowing agreement, the air thick with understanding. The echoes of laughter and collective hopes resonated, giving birth to a unity that felt electrifying.

By the event's conclusion, as the sun dipped below the horizon, a sense of fulfillment settled in their bones. Together, every story, every shared tear, and every laugh stitched a richer fabric woven through time.

Though the void of unlived life lingers, it was merely an invitation, a calling to live passionately and with courage, honoring the dreams of all those lost in the process.

The protagonist left the event with a heart full of gratitude and expectancy. They had embraced the courage to live not only for themselves but in a way that illuminated the lives of others.

They finally understood that while loss had carved a place in their spirit, it was not the essence of who they were. It was merely a chapter in a much larger narrative.

As the sky darkened, soothing calm settled around the protagonist, knowing that the memories of those who had shaped them forever breathed life into their journey, guiding them along the path of courage.

They had learned to celebrate the beauty of life amid heartache; they had discovered that resilience lies not in the absence of grief but in the embrace of all that it meant to exist. Each word penned, each story shared, and every connection made became evidence of the enduring spirit of love, the courage to live embracing both joy and sorrow, illuminating the spaces in between.

Honoring What Could Have Been

As the sun began to set, casting a golden glow over the horizon, the protagonist stood in the quiet solitude of their backyard, contemplating the empty canvas in front of them. It had been a year since they last heard their loved one's laughter, a year since life had shaped itself into a narrative that was suddenly devoid of a vital character. Each day had passed as both an eternity and a blink, filled with echoes of what could have been, memories shared, and dreams left unfulfilled. In this sacred space, the weight of those dreams pressed heavily upon their heart, urging them to confront a poignant truth: the past could not be rewritten, yet its influence could still be felt vibrantly, whispering promises of potential awakenings.

Standing before the small plot of earth that had become a reflection of their shared hopes, the protagonist grasped the shovel, its handle cool against their palm. This was not just an act of gardening; it was a ritual, a commitment to honor their loved one's unrealized potential by nurturing the seeds of their dreams. It was here, in this intimate garden, that they would plant not only flowers and herbs but also the aspirations they had once cultivated together. These dreams had been sprawled across conversations in the soft glow of candlelight, entwined with plans for the future, colorful visions of travel, creativity, and laughter yet to be shared.

The shovel bit into the earth, turning over a patch of soil that had remained untouched for too long. In each scoop, the protagonist dug deeper not just into the ground, but also into the very essence of who they were and the vitality that had flourished with their loved one. Memories danced around them, fleeting yet palpable. They could almost hear the gentle encouragement, the gentle murmur: "You can do this. We can do this together. With every scoop, the protagonist unearthed fragments of their shared past.

There were weekends spent illustrating dreams underneath a sprawling oak tree, evenings tucked away with notebooks, sketches, and ideas that intertwined in vibrant colors. Each pitch of soil seemed to echo with laughter, the delightful chaos of brainstorming, and the promise of future ventures. Those dreams, now just whispers in the wind, deserved to be resurrected through tangible actions, to transcend the boundaries of their lost time.

As they labored, the protagonist felt the layers of their grief peeling away like dormant leaves, exposing the vibrant roots of hope that yearned for nourishment. It was about reclaiming joy amidst the sorrow, about allowing the space of loss to transform into an opportunity for growth. These weren't just flowers meant to adorn the garden; they were symbols of love and belief, external manifestations of a bond that death could not extinguish. Hours passed, marked by the interplay of shadow and light as the sun dipped lower.

After an afternoon of labor, the protagonist knelt beside the freshly turned soil, a heart filled with tender determination. It was time to plant. The basket beside them held a collection of seeds, each carefully chosen to mirror the aspirations they once entertained together. There were sunflowers, tall and bright, symbolizing the light and warmth their love radiated into the world. They had always imagined standing side by side, basking in the glow of their vibrant presence, sharing the beauty of nature while embracing the adventures life offered.

Next were tiny packets of herb seeds, each representing a project they had planned, a cooking class they yearned to attend, infused with laughter and the aromatic scents that would fill their kitchen. There were memories of hand-rolled pasta and roasting vegetables, dreams of creating culinary masterpieces that sparked joy. These were dreams that would materialize, just as fragrant herbs blossomed in the garden, bringing forth the essence of what had once been.

The protagonist whispered heartfelt affirmations with each seed planted. This is for you, for the adventures we dreamed of together. The act of planting became an echo of a promise, a commitment to keep the memory alive by transforming grief into creation. With fingers stained in the rich soil, they crafted a story of life from loss; what had once been a vacuum was now filling with color, growth, and purpose, a tangible proof of their love.

As twilight descended, a gentle breeze rustled the leaves, carrying with it the spirit of their loved one, as if affirming the symbolic nature of the planting. It was a reminder that even amidst the void, their presence remained etched in every aspect of life they had shared. No longer was the past something to mourn; it became a precious muse that inspired future actions and decisions.

Having planted their seeds, they gathered small stones from the nearby stream, arranging them into a heart shape encircling the new patch of earth. Each stone was a tribute, a physical representation of the love that had shaped their journey, the laughter, the tears, and the moments where silence spoke louder than words. They reflected on the narrative that had unfolded over the years, the intertwining paths they had walked, and the beauty that arose from their connection.

Night fell, starlit and serene. In this moment of reflection, the protagonist understood that honoring what could have been meant fully embracing every aspect of the love they had shared. It meant carrying forward the dreams and aspirations that still lingered, finding ways to integrate those sentiments into their life. It became a sacred task, a commitment to not only allowing oneself to grieve but to use that grief as a catalyst for finding joy. It reinforced the belief that love does not fade with absence; it transforms, igniting a fire within that inspires creation and action.

Days turned into weeks, and the garden began to unfold a newfound vibrance, mirroring the protagonist's emotional journey. The seedlings sprouted, breaking through the surface of the soil, defying the darkness that had once surrounded the landscape of their heart. In nurturing these plants, they found their grief transforming from weighty sorrow into an embraceable space of love, recognition, and acceptance. Each growth, each colorful blossom became a reminder that life thrives even in the face of pain.

Every morning, they would spend time tending the vibrant garden, witnessing its evolution. They came to realize that each visit required patience and care not just for the soil and seeds, but within themselves. When thoughts of sadness began to arise, they turned to their garden as a place of solace. They'd pull weeds that represented unfounded guilt or regret, uprooting those feelings to allow their newfound hope to flourish.

Neighbors began to notice the changing landscape, commenting on the beauty that emerged, unaware of the deeper stories concealed within each flower and herb. The protagonist shared snippets of their emotional journey, embodying the very essence of honoring lost relationships. Conversations blossomed, each exchanged word resonating with themes of love, loss, and remembrance. In their vulnerability, they found community, others who, too, had lived amidst the void of unlived lives, each nurturing their own gardens of memories.

As the months continued to pass, the garden grew into a vibrant sanctuary. The sunflowers danced with the rhythm of the wind, their bold yellow heads turning towards the sun, similar to the warmth of the love they once cherished. Culinary herbs peppered the area with rich scents, infusing the air with nostalgia. The protagonist began to experiment with recipes that honored their shared culinary dreams, inviting friends over for dinners that celebrated life amid loss, transforming the heaviness of grief into laughter and shared memories.

These gatherings became a beautiful ritual, blending the flavors of nostalgia with the celebratory spirit of honoring the past. Each plate served represented a memory, spaghetti made from recipes they had once dreamed of crafting together, accompanied by freshly picked basil and thyme that sweetly perfumed the evening air. Friends shared stories, the essence of the departed felt deeply in laughter and anecdotes that knit the past together with the present.

In time, as the summer melted into the warmth of autumn, the protagonist took their journey a step further. Inspired by the abundance in their garden, they decided to launch a small community project, inviting those who had lost loved ones to contribute their own stories, memories, and dreams into a collective garden, a place where each individual could plant a seed honoring their own paths to healing. It was a space that brought together bonds of community, where stories of loss and love merged into a vibrant tapestry of shared resilience.

Each individual who joined brought distinct experiences and dreams, fostering a deeper understanding of the legacy attached to every life lost. The project flourished, blooming into a collective effort that revealed each person's unique journey, creating connections tethered by empathy, hope, and the wish to keep memories alive. It became clear that amidst this chaos of grief, love continually transformed, taking new shapes, flowering blooms that invited warmth into dark spaces.

As autumn arrived and the leaves turned golden and red, the protagonist hosted a gathering in the community garden, so vibrant with life and color. It was a celebration of memories, an evening dedicated to honoring what could have been. As lanterns flickered to life, illuminating the garden's vibrant hues, shared stories resonated among the attendees, their laughter mingled with tears, a healing symphony that ebbed and flowed, embracing the depth of their collective pain.

People came together, exchanging stories of their loved ones, sharing their dreams and aspirations, and intertwining the legacies that filled the void of absence. Through their communal gathering, they recognized that although loss could fracture lives, it also carried the strength to weave connections, bringing forth the beauty of understanding and solidarity.

When it came time to plant their seeds, physical representations of dreams, other attendees decided to include items that symbolized their loved ones alongside the seeds. A paintbrush, a favorite book, a toy, a tangible connection to the past, honoring moments that shaped their stories. As their community gathered to plant each symbol into the earth, they revealed in the beauty of collective grief, allowing it to guide them forward. Each seed planted transformed the garden into a magnificent monument, one that shimmered with echoes of love, legacy, and life.

In that moment of planting together, the protagonist felt an overwhelming sense of gratitude wash over them. They began to understand that the act of honoring what could have been extended beyond an individual experience; it became a collective tapestry of shared resilience and love manifested into action. As seasons passed, what had once begun as a personal mission evolved into a flourishing garden of hope and enduring memory, a living testimony to lives intertwined in love.

Each bloom, every sprout stood as a reminder of dreams and connections that endured beyond the confines of loss. The protagonist learned to nourish their own garden of reflection and allow joy to overcome grief in its many forms, recognizing that every flower carried a piece of the past, woven into the expansive story of life. Ultimately, they discovered that the journey of honoring a loved one was not merely an act of memory, but a transformation, a metamorphosis that reshaped grief into purpose.

The past could never disappear, nor could it be rewritten; instead, it became a powerful motivator, compelling them to embrace life's beauty, to find warmth amid the void, initiated by love's enduring spirit. Flashbacks of laughter danced in their memories, echoing promises of dreams that would continue to bloom, whispering softly through the garden's flourishing path. Even in absence, love had proven its remarkable ability to inspire action, tethering the weight of loss into the expansive gardens of honor and hope, reminding the protagonist and all others that healing was a possibility, nurtured within the unity of shared dreams and the recognition of lives well-lived. In this space, they could transform grief into legacy, continually finding ways to honor what could have been with every seed sown.

Serenade of the Stars

A Night of Reflection

The night unfolded like a dark velvet tapestry, dotted with brilliant pinpricks of light. The protagonist, feeling the cool grass beneath their feet, lay back and let the wonders of the universe wash over them. The stars shimmered overhead, their glow illuminating the vastness of the sky, casting a celestial glow on the world below. It was a breathtaking spectacle, one that seemed to promise clarity amidst the chaos of life. As they gazed upward, a gentle breeze whispered through the trees, carrying the secrets of the cosmos and lulling them into deep contemplation.

In that moment of stillness, surrounded by nature's beauty, the protagonist found a refuge from life's turmoil. The shimmering stars felt like countless eyes watching over them, each one a witness to the stories of humanity. Each glimmer held a history, an existence tethered to dreams, hopes, and losses. They remembered the nights spent with loved ones, laughter echoing beneath the infinite sky, and the quiet conversations that lingered long after the stars had faded into the dawn. It was as if the universe had cast a net of introspection around them, drawing their thoughts into a cosmic whirlpool. In this vast tapestry of existence, the protagonist contemplated their own life, feeling both minuscule and immensely significant. The grandeur of the stars could dwarf them, yet each flickering light felt like a thread connecting back to their own essence. The universe was a reminder of life's interconnectedness. Stars had once collapsed, birthing new worlds, while the stories of those who had come before laid the groundwork for who they were today.

The protagonist mused on how every action, every choice, rippled through the cosmos, influencing the lives of others in ways they might never fully comprehend. In a life marked by fleeting relationships and transient moments, the ties that bound them to others felt both fragile and infinite.

As they shifted their gaze to constellations, each formation represented something ancient, a mythology recounted time and again. There was Orion, the hunter, eternally pursuing his prey, a dance that echoed themes of ambition and desire. The protagonist found solace in his relentless chase, recognizing that they too had been swept up in their own pursuits, sometimes at the cost of genuine connection. Had they become so entangled in their aspirations that they had lost sight of the people surrounding them, those stars of their own existence? The cosmos was an arena for all human emotion; the poignant reminders of loss shimmered just as brightly as the symbols of hope. For every star that burned brightly, there were others that had extinguished long before, leaving only memories.

The protagonist thought of loved ones who had passed, their lives now woven into the very fabric of the universe. Those stars may have become shadows, but they continued to inspire, illuminating the paths of their remaining family and friends. Thoughts began to swirl, tender yet heavy, pressing on their heart. The memories of miscommunication and unfulfilled desires floated through their mind like echoes of distant laughter. Each unresolved moment tangled with the light of distant suns, urging the protagonist to confront the emotional gravity that hung over their relationships. In this vast expanse, amplified by the silence of the night, they understood that mourning could coexist with moments of ultimate peace. The stars, ever watchful, seemed to invite both sorrow and gratitude. Nestled in this serenity, comfort washed over them, reminding the protagonist that grief and joy were allies in the human journey.

They took a deep breath, allowing the crisp night air to fill their lungs, understanding that uncertainty was as natural as the stars that twinkled above. Life's unpredictability echoed within the boundless sky, teaching lessons about trusting the journey even when the destination remained unclear. In this sanctuary away from worldly distractions, the protagonist pondered their purpose in the great weave of life. The night sky invited an exploration of identity, a reflection of who they had been and who they might still become. The questions lingered like heavy constellations: What would their legacy be? How would they be remembered? Amongst the stars, these thoughts took on an expansive quality, illuminating their mind like the celestial light above.

As time flowed gently like the river of stars, the protagonist became mesmerized by their reflections. They envisioned lives unfolding across the fabric of time and space. Each individual was a solitary star, their light merging with others to create constellations of shared experiences. Together, they formed galaxies, families, friendships, and communities crafted from love and loss. Gazing toward the constellation of Cassiopeia, they recalled stories of resilience, tales of triumph over adversity, and the strength found in vulnerability. Each curve of the constellation served as a metaphor for the human experience the irregularities and imperfections that made everyone truly breathtaking. There was grace in the struggles endured, in the moments when love won over hate, and when compassion stretched towards those in need.

The protagonist's thoughts shifted, pondering the nature of memories. Were they flickering stars in the night sky, guiding people through dark times? Each cherished recollection felt like fuel for the soul, an ember igniting warmth within their hearts. The connections created throughout life transformed mundane moments into lasting legacies, stories that would be recounted over campfires and in quiet homes, illuminating future generations. Redefining their relationship with the stars, the protagonist smiled, realizing how important it was to cherish the fleeting moments shared with others. Every smile exchanged, every handheld, and every word spoken became part of that starry canopy overhead. Goodbyes did not erase those connections; they merely transformed, creating ethereal constellations that continued to shine through the darkness.

Suddenly welled within was an overwhelming sense of gratitude. Life might be a fragile balance struck against the backdrop of eternity, but it also overflowed with heartfelt joy born from love. The connections established gave rise to a strength that endured, making each individual's existence meaningful in the grand scheme of creation.

As the stars twinkled against the blackness of night, the protagonist felt resolved to focus on love and remembrance. The realization solidified that family lines extend beyond the grave; a legacy of love presents long after physical bodies are buried to the ground. The protagonist visualized those timeless spirits dancing among the stars, weaving in and out of constellations. Instead of diminishing with distance, the relationships would continue to grow, thriving as living stories passed from one generation to the next. The accretive nature of time created an opportunity for healing. It was not merely about moving past heartaches but allowing oneself to experience those emotions fully loss, joy, despair, and hope, knowing that they made the tapestry of existence richer.

The protagonist let out a soft sigh, with every exhale releasing past burdens and inhaling gentle acceptance. They comprehended the transformative power within that cycle. In those contemplative minutes under the stars, the protagonist uncovered a treasure trove of understanding. They recognized an innate drive to share stories to pass on wisdom cultivated through experience. The urgency to live fully blossomed from their reflections. Life was precious, a precious tapestry interwoven with fleeting moments that deserved to be cherished. As if summoning the strength of the starlight itself, they felt empowered to act with authenticity, to express feelings, and to take risks in relationships without fear of loss. Each connection forged would ultimately enrich the lives of others, reverberating across time and space like the celestial dance above.

With renewed vigor, the protagonist sat up, scanning the sky for shooting stars and making wishes as they sent heartfelt messages into the universe. They would honor their loved ones, uphold their legacies, and share stories that bore witness to stubborn love and enduring hope. In each wish cast into the vast unknown, they felt a symbiosis emerge: a giving back to the universe that had gifted them life. As the night wore on, constellations shifted. In the expansion of twilight towards early dawn, the protagonist felt a sense of urgency to awaken the world. This was a fleeting moment of connection with eternity, and they did not want to forget the lessons imparted by the luminous stars. They sensed that a world was ready for those willing to navigate the dark together, opting for connection over solitude, vulnerability over apathy.

The quiet enchantment of the night slowly gave way to the golden hues of morning as dawn broke; the protagonist remained steadfast under the light of hope bursting on the horizon. Each dawn signals new beginnings, a reminder that life endlessly renews itself, even against the shadows of night. Seeds of intention planted during midnight reflections took root, illuminating paths forward. They felt compelled to share the experience, to recall the night spent with the stars illuminating the journey ahead. Every person encountered their star, each cast connection forming bonds that transcended time and distance. There was a warmth suffusing their spirit, igniting a flame that would guide them forward. In every heartbeat, in every breath taken, they sensed eternity whispering to them, shaping a future grounded in love and honor.

The universe sang its melody, and the protagonist felt a thrill. Life was a magnificent journey waiting to unfold, with the stars watching over to light the way.

Whispers of the Cosmos

As the protagonist gazes into the night, the vast expanse of the cosmos unfolds above them, a glittering tapestry of stars. Each twinkle feels like a whisper, a secret carried down from the celestial realm and steeped in mystery. They stand in awe, captivated by the sheer beauty of the night sky, where innumerable points of light seem to pulsate in rhythm with their heartbeat. It is in this tranquil moment that they begin to sense the stars communicating stories from beyond, echoing tales woven into the fabric of existence, connecting their solitary life to a grander narrative, a narrative shared by countless souls throughout time.

In this stillness, surrounded by the quiet rustle of leaves and the cool embrace of night air, the protagonist engages in a silent dialogue with the cosmos. They contemplate the shimmering stars, contemplating how ancient cultures viewed constellations as guides and storytellers, celestial markers that shaped human understanding of the universe. Throughout history, people have looked up to these distant suns, attributing meanings and mythologies to each formation, drawing connections between the heavens and the earth. The night sky becomes a canvas populated by the legacy of humanity's collective imagination.

The protagonist recalls how, in various mythologies, stars were seen as messengers of the lost, shining down to remind the living of those who had journeyed beyond. In Greek mythology, for instance, the soul of a departed loved one would find solace among the stars, becoming a star themselves, eternally shimmering in the vastness of the sky. They think of Orion, whose story is deeply intertwined with themes of love, loss, and heroism, a recounting of how he became a constellation after his tragic demise.

As the protagonist takes in this narrative, the cosmos transforms from mere distant lights into guardians of memory, holding fragments of lost lives and their stories. Each constellation evokes memories of love shared and lives lived, illustrating the ethereal connection between earth and sky. The protagonist feels the weight of their own losses. They think of the loved ones who have become stars, remarkable individuals whose spirits linger in the vastness, guiding and protecting those they left behind. It is a poignant realization, one that bridges the gap between life and death, weaving losses into a continuum of existence that encompasses the past and present. The stars become symbols of hope, illuminating the darkness as reminders that death is not a finite end but a transformation, a journey into another realm.

Amidst this reflection, the protagonist's thoughts drift to the rich tapestry of cultural interpretations regarding the stars. In many Indigenous cultures, stars are revered as ancestors or spirits guiding their descendants. The protagonists envision gatherings under the night sky, where stories are shared around blazing fires and wisdom is passed down through generations. Each constellation serves as a marker of heritage and shared identity, each star a note in the collective symphony of human experience. The protagonist feels a sense of belonging amid this cosmic community, understanding that they are part of a larger weave, a thread connecting to those who came before and those who will follow.

In South Asian cultures, the stars are often intertwined with the idea of fate and destiny, emphasizing the belief that the universe conspires to shape individual paths. The protagonist thinks of how horoscopes, tied to celestial movements, have historically provided insights into human lives, suggesting that every person carries a piece of the universe within them. The stars thus become not only symbols of connection but also agents of meaning, imbuing existence with purpose.

As they gaze up, the protagonist understands that they, too, are a constellation, a unique amalgamation of experiences, dreams, and memories shaped by the cosmos' design. Each flickering light now radiates an energy that resonates with the protagonist's own heartbeat, an echo of love and longing that transcends the barriers of existence. They close their eyes momentarily, allowing the memories of those lost to surface clearly, each one laden with lessons learned and moments cherished. The act of remembering becomes intertwined with the rhythm of the stars, and the protagonist imagines each loved one gazing down at them. The memories held within those stars interlace with their identity in a dance of continuity, revealing that love does not dissipate; it transforms, evolving into a vibrant thread woven into the protagonist's very being.

The night deepens, and the stars gleam like tiny diamonds scattered across a velvet backdrop. The protagonist opens their eyes, feeling a sense of stillness that belies the tumult of feelings within. With each breath, they draw in the timeless stories and wisdom encapsulated in the starry expanse. The universe hums with life, resonating with the memories of those who grieved and celebrated, creating a profound sense of connection that transcends time and space. In this moment, the protagonist begins to understand that grief is a witness to love, a love that refuses to be extinguished. They realize that acknowledging their sorrow also means honoring the depth of their affection for those they have lost. Just as the stars navigate the night sky, illuminating the darkness, love serves as a beacon guiding them through their own despair. Memories now become luminous threads, weaving a tapestry that weaves together hope and loss, illustrating an intricate and beautiful narrative of a life well-lived.

The protagonist begins to ponder the implications of this realization. What if every person lived their life as a star, illuminating the path for others even when they were no longer physically present? What if each individual's story could serve as a guiding light, a reminder that moments of joy and sorrow are interconnected? The notion becomes invigorating empowering them to embrace their journey and the legacy they would ultimately leave behind. They imagine themselves not merely as a solo act but as part of a chorus that echoes through the ages, a part of the ongoing serenade of existence.

As they gaze deeper into the cosmos, stars transform into symbols of unity, each one standing indivisible from the collective experience of humanity. The protagonist realizes they carry within themselves a multitude of stories, moments shaped by laughter and tears, love and loss. They feel compelled to add their voice to the fabric of existence, to contribute to the shared narrative that transcends time. The guiding stars invite them to embrace their vulnerability, to speak openly about their grief and joy, fostering a sense of kinship with others. The darkness cloak transformed into a rich symphony of emotion, each star reflecting laughter from joyful gatherings, warmth from heartfelt embraces, and the sorrow of farewells whispered into the night.

The protagonist allows themselves to be moved by these emotions, acknowledging the blend of feelings that define the human experience. They realize love is both timeless and fleeting, mirroring the cycles of life and death, joy and sorrow. In each moment of connection, there lies the possibility of healing and understanding, a dawning recognition that the beauty of shared memory can bridge the chasms formed by loss. By embracing the whispers of the cosmos, the protagonist comprehends the need for connection even amid isolation. They sense an inner calling to reach out, to build bonds that span across generations. Inspired by the symbolism of the stars overlooking them, they believe in the importance of storytelling, of connecting lives through shared experiences and memories. Confronting the challenges of loss head-on, they consider how their journey can inspire others navigating their grief, lighting the way forward in a world marked by uncertainty.

As they breathe in the crisp night air, each inhale infused with stardust, the protagonist feels the essence of empathy taking root within them. They recognize the universality of loss, the shared experience that binds humanity together, reminding them that they are never truly alone. The stars serve as a comforting presence, their illuminating glow a powerful reminder that memories persist long after those we love are gone, present within us like constellations in the night sky.

Through this realization, a renewed sense of purpose emerges. The protagonist begins to contemplate their legacy; the impact of their existence intertwined with those they love. They feel empowered to create a narrative of hope, rooted in connection and understanding. This journey involves embracing vulnerability and acknowledging the profound sweetness in the acts of remembrance, moments that reflect the love, laughter, and resilience that accompany all lives.

As the night deepens, the glow of the stars continues to illuminate their heart, reminding them that the cosmos is ever-pulsing with life, forever containing the whispers of those who came before. With each blink, each shimmering light, sparks of inspiration arise driving home the idea that life and death are not distinct endpoints but threads in an infinite tapestry woven together by love, loss, and hope. The protagonist feels buoyed by these realizations. They vow to honor their loved ones, allowing their memories to guide their actions, foster connections, and inspire future generations. Drawn by an overwhelming sense of belonging, they sit quietly, gazing up at the celestial bodies, a multitude of stories unfolding with each flicker. Here, they are reminded of the fragility and beauty of life, of how each fleeting moment builds a cosmos of experience, woven from tears and laughter, shadows and light, endings and new beginnings.

In this sense of unity, they come to know that the whispers of the stars are not just echoes of the past but seeds of inspiration that will continue to grow, intertwined with those who remain and those who journey onward. In this cosmic embrace, the protagonist solidifies their conviction that while they may traverse the depths of grief and solitude, they are forever linked to an infinite universe of stories. Each star glimmers with the essence of those departed, illuminating paths yet to be traveled while serving as constant reminders of the love that remains. These connections enrich the fabric of existence, urging the protagonist forward with hope and a promise that love indeed transcends time and space.

With newfound clarity and purpose, the protagonist rises from their contemplative stance, feeling invigorated by the symphony of life surrounding them. They take one last glance at the stars and make a solemn vow to carry forth the love intertwined with the whispers of the cosmos. With the night sky as their witness, they embrace the interconnectedness of existence, knowing that as long as the stars shine brightly overhead, the stories of those who touch our lives will echo forever.

The Dance of Life

The sky above was a vast canvas, painted in deep shades of indigo and sprinkled with shimmering stars. Each twinkle seemed to pulse with life, whispering secrets of the universe that stirred something deep within the protagonist. As they lay on the cool grass, a soft breeze caressing their skin, the world felt both expansive and intimate, as if every soul on Earth was somehow connected through the celestial dance overhead.

Tonight was a special night; one the protagonist had been eagerly awaiting since the echoes of loss had first resonated in their heart. The starlight promised not just comfort, but a celebration of memories shared among those who had departed; a communion of lives interconnected through joy, laughter, and sorrow. With a flicker of hope igniting within, the protagonist had invited their friends and family to join in a stargazing ritual, hoping it would help them all find solace in shared experiences.

As dusk deepened into night, the familiar faces began to gather in the garden, each person carrying a unique story woven into the fabric of their life. The protagonist welcomed them with open arms, feeling a warmth enveloping them as they exchanged quiet smiles and comforting embraces. The air buzzed with anticipation, rich with the promise of shared reverie. Blankets were spread out on the lush, verdant grass, transforming the space into a sanctum of remembrance. The gentle murmurs of voices filled the atmosphere, each participant settling into the circle, forming a tapestry woven together by threads of connection and understanding. Familiar scents of blooming flowers blended with the cool night air, creating a sensory layer to the unfolding experience.

The protagonist reclined back on the blanket, drawing in a deep breath as they gazed up at the myriads of stars. The constellations twinkled defiantly against the backdrop of an eternal sky, silently bearing witness to the stories that had unfolded beneath them. "Look! There's Orion!" one of the guests exclaimed, pointing toward the formation of stars.

Instantly, a wave of memories washed over the group stories of childhood adventures, of nights spent outdoors looking for shapes in the sky, and of elder relatives who had taught them the names of the stars. Each revelation sparked laughter and murmurs of nostalgia, connecting them through the fabric of time. The protagonist felt the tension within their heart begin to ease; here, in the shared light of the cosmos, grief was refracted into something brighter.

One by one, the participants began sharing their own memories inspired by the stars. A woman named Claire began, her voice tinged with tenderness, recounting how her grandmother would take her stargazing on warm summer nights. "She would tell me stories about the constellations, how they came to be, how they held the dreams of those who had passed," she said, her eyes sparkling with unshed tears. With each story shared, the collective energy transformed the atmosphere. As everyone connected through their shared histories, loss began to feel less isolating. The protagonist found solace in Claire's words, realizing how the stories of others were often mirrors reflecting their own experiences flashes of light in the dark, guiding them through the night.

Next, a man named Raj spoke up, his voice steady yet reverent. "For me, the stars remind me of my father," he shared, pausing to collect his thoughts. "He was a sailor, spent most nights at sea. He would always tell me that the stars were his navigators. When I look at them now, I can almost hear his voice guiding me, a lighthouse in the dark waters of life. The heartfelt confession resonated within the group, and the shift was palpable. Grief transformed into connection through shared narratives. As Raj continued, he remarked that his father used to say that loss is part of life's voyage, navigating the visible and the invisible, much like the stars that guide him home. His story hung in the air, a testament to love's enduring power beyond physical presence. The protagonist cherished these moments, watching as emotions surged and receded, like the tides echoing the rhythms of life and loss. Each shared story acted as a thread, knitting them together amidst their individual grief.

There was something so evident in that moment: the realization that they were not alone in their battles. Grief, like the universe, was vast, yet they found themselves tethered to one another in the most beautiful of ways. As narratives sprang forth one after another, the starlit sky above mirrored the hearts below, twinkling with memories, laughter, and echoes of lives that had touched theirs in profound ways. Melissa, a friend who had recently lost her sister, spoke next. "I used to dream of her when we were little kids, how we would fly through the stars, leaving a trail of sparkles behind us. When I see the stars, I feel her with me, a guide through the darkest of nights. I've learned that she hasn't really left; she dances among the stars, reminding me to find joy, no matter the sorrows I carry. Her words painted the night with vibrant colors; this revelation stirred the emotions in others, and soon participants shared how they felt their loved ones among the shimmering bodies in the cosmos.

A newfound understanding emerged among the group while each sorrow was unique, the bonds they shared helped illuminate the path ahead, guiding them through the veils of grief and into the embrace of connection. The stargazing continued, stories spiraling around the circle, much as the stars glittered in the sky. The conversations flowed easily; the initial hesitance swept away by the magic of remembrance. The protagonist felt it best summed up in a phrase shared by Julio, a lifelong friend. "When we are bereaved, we often feel shattered, and in those moments, it is important to remember that those pieces can create new patterns of beauty. Like constellations, our lives create connections, weaving tales that transcend time and space. This idea resonated deeply, weaving its way into the fabric of their gathering, shifting it into something soulful. They were weaving together a cosmic tapestry of emotions and memories, where joy and grief entwined, celebrated as part of the human experience.

The protagonist felt a spark deep within, driven by the collective gratitude that illuminated the night, comforting in its essence. Overhead, a shooting star dashed across the sky, a fleeting moment echoing hope. It was a reminder of the impermanence that defined existence yet also evoked dreams that lingered on. The protagonist let out a soft gasp, drawing everyone's gaze toward the brilliance above, all hearts beating as one under the celestial display. It felt as if time stopped, allowing a moment of collective silence, a sacred pause to honor the weight of dreams, wishes, and losses unspoken.

As the eventide gathered around them, the protagonist took a deep breath, feeling lighter but also deeply aware of the emotional load they had all carried. Finally, they spoke, their voice quiet yet imbued with intensity. "Thank you for coming tonight and sharing these memories, for being a part of this stargazing ritual. It reminds us that, amid all that we have lost, we are not alone. The stars shine on, and so do we, within and through each other's stories. Grief is deeply personal, but in these connections, I find comfort during dark times, and I hope you do too.

As they concluded their thoughts, a collective warmth radiated among the group, binding them like constellations painted across the cosmic canvas. Fear had effortlessly transformed into connection; sorrow had turned to understanding. The night stretched on, filled with laughter, stories, and ethereal beauty, each shared moment echoing the timeless dance of vulnerability and love that wove them together. The ritual lingered long into the night, the stars offering their eternal embrace, cradling the stories shared and memories created. Each participant contributed their vivid hues to the tapestry, reminding the protagonist of life's intricacy, how the fabric of existence can be both heartbreakingly beautiful and overwhelmingly difficult. In that sacred space, they found the courage to face the duality of loss existing side by side with the love that once was, upheld by the connections nurtured among those still present.

As the gathering drew to a close, the group carefully exchanged hugs and warm farewells, the flickering of their emotional connections echoing well beyond the physical space. The protagonist felt buoyed, carrying within them a piece of everyone they had shared that intimate evening with, and their stories would forever twinkle in the night sky alongside the stars. Leaving the garden, the protagonist glanced back, stealing one last look at the sky, a magnificent blur of splendor that felt alive. They felt an overwhelming sense of gratitude, a promise that, while grief is intensely personal, the love shared among us in life can persist and illuminate our paths, guiding us even through the darkest of nights.

And as they stepped into the world beyond, armed with the

collective strength of those they held dear, the protagonist felt forever changed, ready to embrace both the sorrow and the beauty that life continued to unfold like a tapestry above them, forever dancing in the embrace of the stars.

Closure in the Chaos

Embracing Life's Unpredictability

The air was thick with anticipation as the protagonist stepped into a world altered by the whims of unforeseen chaos. Life's framework, once rigid and predictable, now lay crumbled at their feet, replaced by a swirling vortex of confusion and anxiety. What had started as a typical Tuesday had morphed into a day that would echo in the corners of their memory, forever marked by the lessons it would unveil.

As the morning sun poured through the curtains, a peculiar stillness hung in the air. It was the calm before the storm, a deceptive tranquility that would soon be shattered. The protagonist clutched their mug of coffee, watching steam rise and dissipate, much like the semblance of control they had managed to maintain. It struck them how swiftly life could flip itself upside down, turning mundane familiarity into a tangled web of uncertainties.

In the middle of a busy street, the protagonist's phone buzzed relentlessly in their pocket. The vibrations felt like tiny bursts of anxiety, prickling at the edges of their calm. They could sense the tension building inside, like a pressure cooker ready to explode. With a deep breath, they fished the phone from their pocket, glancing at the screen with a mix of hope and dread. The message was from their partner a text delivered in cold, concise language that's belonging to the world in emergency. "We need to talk. It's important. Can we meet?" The words bounced around in their mind like angry hornets, stinging with implications they didn't yet want to confront. Life, in its unpredictable nature, appeared to be crumbling, if only for a fleeting moment. Having built their existence on the solidity of routine and predictable outcomes, the protagonist felt roots of anxiety sprouting deep within. The neat compartments of their life work, relationships, personal aspirations began to feel suffocatingly fragile. How had things spiraled so quickly into a maelstrom of uncertainty?

As they made their way to the café where they agreed to meet, the bustling city seemed to mock their struggle. Laughter and conversations filled the air, infusing the atmosphere with a vibrance that felt foreign to their current state of mind. Each step was heavy, grounded by the weight of the unknown that loomed ahead. The unpredictability embraced them; it whispered stories of countless others navigating the same chaotic landscape, yet they felt achingly alone in their turmoil.

Entering the café, the clatter of cups and the rich aroma of freshly brewed coffee enveloped them. They spotted their partner seated at a corner table; their face clouded with an expression that hinted at the stormy conversation brewing. The protagonist's heart raced, drumming out a frantic rhythm as they settled into the seat across from them. "They found a lump," their partner said, the words heavy enough to disrupt the air between them. "I have a doctor's appointment tomorrow. They might be..." A deep breath broke the sentence, leaving a chasm of uncertainty hanging between them. No further words were needed; the gravity of the situation spun a web of dread.

In that moment, the protagonist felt as though the ground beneath them had vanished entirely. The café blurred into the background; even the bustling patrons faded into obscurity. All they could grasp was the suffocating silence of the unknown, the chaos that was now intricately woven into their life. For the protagonist, the world outside became a distant echo as they focused inward, spiraling deep into the recesses of their mind. The days that followed unfolded like a disjointed film, with scenes spinning chaotically, no regard for structure. Appointments were made, consultations set, and life felt like an out-of-control roller-coaster. The unpredictability of the situation gripped them, magnifying every emotion: the fear of the unknown, the anxiety of waiting, and the unbearable ache of what a worried mind could conceive. The hours lost their meaning, and time bent in ways that felt distortive. Days seemed to stretch into eternity, yet they were also fleeting, slipping away from the protagonist like sand through their fingers. They clung desperately to fragments of routine working out early, finishing task lists, and trying to maintain a sense of normalcy. Yet all around, chaos reigned, undermining efforts to stabilize the world outside. Negative thoughts swirled endlessly; questions twisted into an intricate knot: What if the diagnosis was severe? What if treatments failed? Each question added weight to an already burdened heart. The mind spiraled further into dark corners, into territory where hope, frailly flickering amidst the onslaught of fear, dwelt.

But amid the chaos, whispers of calm started to surface. Memories of quiet moments began breaking the suffocating hold of anxiety. They were simple things: sipping tea on the porch, laughter floating through a shared meal, and the comfort of a soft embrace. Pictures of the everyday emerged like rays of sun breaking through dark clouds, nudging the protagonist to remember that beauty is intertwined with uncertainty.

One evening, the protagonist found solace in nature. They stepped into a nearby park, inhaling deeply and absorbing the ambiance, the rustle of leaves above, the distant sounds of children playing, and the gentle chirping of birds welcoming twilight. Nature had an uncanny ability to remind them of life's enduring rhythm, its unpredictable essence, both terrifying and beautiful. As they wandered through the garden trails, the weight of uncertainties began to lift. The protagonist realized that, just as seasons flowed seamlessly from one to the next, life too ebbed and flowed in patterns that refused to yield to predictability.

It was this notion of conformity that had brought them comfort, but it was also the source of dread. Sitting on a weathered bench under the embrace of a grand oak tree, they let their thoughts cascade freely, a catharsis of sorts. They recognized that chaos was a natural part of existence, a reminder that life was not always about control but rather about navigating the unknown with grace. Perhaps in embracing unpredictability, they could open a window to the beauty that came with it.

A series of meditative breaths drew them to a moment of clarity. It dawned on them that embracing life's unpredictable nature meant holding space for both joy and sorrow. Happiness and pain could coexist, weaving an intricate tapestry of life experiences. This realization sparked a flicker of resilience, drawing them from the shadows of despair into a space ripe for growth. The following days were not devoid of challenges. Appointments brought news that triggered emotions like tidal waves, yet amidst the chaos, the protagonist sought those moments of calm, anchoring themselves whenever possible. They began to recognize the power of shared vulnerability. Conversations with friends unfolded as they opened up about the whirlwind of emotions spinning out of their control, offering them a sense of camaraderie that lessened the burden they felt.

One rainy afternoon, sitting on their front porch, they connected with a childhood friend. The nostalgia, combined with shared laughter and storytelling, instilled a peacefulness that reminded the protagonist of the essential role of human connection amid chaos. They talked about the unpredictability of life, and both shared stories of loss and moments of transformative hope, weaving experiences that only deepened their bond. Slowly, they began to redefine their narrative around unpredictability, no longer seeing it merely as something to be feared, but as a catalyst propelling them into the depths of self-discovery and exploration. They optimistically embraced the strange beauty that emerged when schedules disintegrated, and life took unexpected turns. Accepting unpredictability as an integral facet of existence opened up a world of new possibilities. With every challenge they encountered, the protagonist learned to pivot, adapt, and seek clarity in murky waters. They found themselves leaning into uncertainty rather than resisting it, recognizing how often life took unexpected yet rich forms for growth. If one thread unraveled, they could explore new patterns, creating a life tapestry woven from resilience, hope, and acceptance. Guided by this newfound perspective, the protagonist forged ahead, ready to embrace whatever the future held. They accepted that life's true essence lay not merely in its predictability but in the vibrant hues of uncertainty, offering newfound clarity amidst swirling storms.

As they ventured forth, each moment a reminder of the interconnected needlepoint of existence, they saw unpredictability for what it was: a chance for deeper discovery, for heartwarming connections, and for finding joy in the messiness of life. In the following weeks, they began writing down their experiences, each word transforming painful chaos into poetry. It became therapeutic, allowing them to relive moments of calm amidst the storm and to find beauty in the complex fabric of human experience. Through writing moments of raw honesty, they navigated the labyrinth of emotions that accompanied their journey, empowering others through the shared vulnerability that connected them all.

Through this exploration, they discovered that embracing life's unpredictability did not erase pain; rather, it contextualized it within a broader narrative of existence. It opened pathways toward gratitude and toward celebrating love's endurance even when faced with uncertainty. And so, weaving their stories into everyday conversations, the protagonist found lightness in their journey, hopeful for the future. Life's unpredictability became an intricate dance, a melody that softened the harsh notes of chaos with harmonies of resilience and acceptance. Each day held a promise: the gift of being alive amid the mysteries of existence. Herein lay the beauty the chaos did not define them; it was merely one thread woven into the rich tapestry of their life. Emotions may ebb and flow, but through it all lay the undeniable truth that every twist and turn would sculpt and guide their journey forward, into the arms of the unpredictable yet wondrous tapestry of being human.

Finding Solace in Disarray

The rain fell in rhythmic torrents, each drop a relentless reminder of life's unpredictability. The sky was a blanket of gray, heavy and thick with clouds that seemed to press down on the world below. In the midst of this chaos, the protagonist, Samuel, found himself wandering the streets, seeking refuge from both the storm and the internal chaos that had taken root in his heart after the loss of his mother. With every step, he felt the weight of his grief pressing against him, dragging him down like the saturated earth beneath his feet. As he turned a corner, the soft glow of a small café beckoned him. The sign outside read "The Gathering Place," a cozy name that intrigued him amidst the storm's tumult. Samuel pushed open the heavy door, and a wave of warmth enveloped him, wrapping around him like a comforting embrace. The smell of freshly brewed coffee and the sound of gentle chatter filled the air, creating a stark contrast to the chaos outside. He stepped inside, seeking a moment's peace, hoping to drown out the discord in his heart.

As he settled into a corner table, he noticed the eclectic decor that adorned the café. Vintage photographs lined the walls, capturing moments of laughter and joy, each telling a story that felt distant yet familiar. A group of friends engaged in animated conversation at a nearby table, their laughter punctuating the air like music. He couldn't help but smile, despite the heaviness that lingered just beneath the surface. It was then that a young woman approached his table, her curly hair bouncing with energy and a bright smile lighting up her face. "Is this seat taken?" she asked, motioning to the chair opposite him. A part of Samuel wanted to refuse her company, to keep cocooned in his solitude, but something in her eyes urged him to welcome her.

"No, please, have a seat," he replied, gestured to the chair. "I'm Clara," she said, extending her hand with an infectious enthusiasm.

Samuel took her hand, feeling an unexpected warmth in the simple touch. Samuel. "Nice to meet you," he replied, trying to muster a smile.

"So, what brings you out on a day like this? Are you trying to escape the chaos, too?" she asked, eyeing the rain-lashed window behind him.

Samuel hesitated, unsure of how much to reveal about the storm raging within. He took a breath and decided to share a fraction of his truth. "Just needed to get out of my head for a bit. The weather feels a lot like how I've been feeling lately. Just… chaotic."

Clara nodded, her expression shifting to one of understanding. "I get it. Life can be overwhelming sometimes. But sometimes, chaos leads to the most beautiful moments, don't you think?" Her voice was soothing, and for the first time in days, he felt a flicker of hope ignite in the dim corners of his heart.

"What do you mean?" he asked, genuinely intrigued.

She leaned in, her eyes sparkling with mischief. "Let me tell you a story. I used to be in a band, and we had this one gig in a tiny bar during a thunderstorm. The power went out, leaving us in complete darkness. Instead of packing up and leaving, we started playing an acoustic set by candlelight, and it turned into the most magical night. People danced in the rain outside, and the chaos turned into a celebration of music and life. It was beautiful."

Samuel could visualize the scene she described, the laughter, the music blending with the storm's rhythm. He found solace in her words, embracing the idea that even in chaos, there are hidden gems waiting to be discovered.

As they continued to talk, Clara shared her own experiences. She spoke of her family, who had recently moved away, leaving her feeling lost and disconnected. But instead of wallowing in loneliness, she chose to create a community in the city, a patchwork of friends from different backgrounds, all united by their shared experiences and stories. "It's like finding our own little family in the chaos of the world, you know?" she said, her excitement infectious. "We have potlucks, game nights, and even spontaneous dance parties! You should join us sometime!"

His heart warmed at the invitation, and for the first time since his mother's death, he didn't feel completely alone. The thought of laughter, music, and connection kindled hope within him, lighting the dark corners of his grief.

Before they parted ways, Clara asked him for his number, insisting she would reach out about the next gathering. As he stepped back into the rain, he felt lighter, as if Clara's laughter had washed away some of the heaviness that clung to him. The chaos around him remained, but he began to see it through a new lens, one where connection and resilience could flourish. Over the next few days, Samuel found himself thinking about Clara and the stories she shared. A new resolve settled in him; perhaps he could face the chaos of his life with the same courage she had shown. On impulse, he decided to attend the next gathering Clara mentioned.

The night of the gathering arrived, and he stood outside the door of a small apartment, his heart racing. The sounds of laughter and music wafted through the air, both inviting and intimidating at the same time. He hesitated for a moment but then took a deep breath and knocked. The door swung open, revealing Clara's radiant smile. "You made it!" she exclaimed, pulling him in with an enthusiastic hug. As he stepped into the warmth of the space, he was enveloped by the vibrant energy radiating from the group of friends gathered inside. The aroma of home-cooked food and the joyous sounds of conversation wrapped around him like a comforting blanket.

As he moved through the gathering, Samuel was introduced to everyone, each person bringing their own story, their own chaos.

Laughter erupted as they shared anecdotes of their lives, moments of resilience often punctuated by humor. He felt something begin to shift within him as he listened to their stories, which mirrored his own in unexpected ways. There was Lila, who had just exited a tumultuous relationship and was determined to rediscover herself. She shared her hilarious misadventures in dating, turning her heartbreak into comedic tales that had everyone in stitches.

Then there was Tony, who had lost his job and struggled to make ends meet, but instead of despairing, he showcased his talents as a budding chef, dazzling everyone with a delicious meal he had prepared. His passion and creativity shone through, and it dawned upon Samuel that even in financial disarray, Tony was forging connections through the art of food.

As the night continued, the chaos of life transformed into a symphony of shared experiences. They played games, mixing competitive spirit with laughter, and even danced in the living room, letting the music guide them as they moved together, forgetting their worries for a while. Around midnight, as everyone began to wind down, Clara gathered the group for a final toast. "To the chaos!" she declared, raising her glass high. "To the connections we find within it!" Samuel lifted his glass among them, feeling a swell of gratitude. The warmth of their camaraderie settled deep within him, reminding him of the human capacity for resilience, even amidst chaos. In that flash of joy, he realized the chaos didn't have to be a burden he carried alone.

Through these meaningful connections, he discovered pockets of solace woven through his grief, comforting few moments that reminded him to find laughter in the storm. The following weeks were a whirlwind of laughter, shared meals, and new friendships. Samuel found himself actively engaging in the chaos of life rather than retreating from it. Although the grief of his loss lingered like a shadow, he began to accept it as part of his life tapestry rather than something that solely defined him.

One evening, as he sat among friends, he recounted stories of his mother, memories that had previously been too painful to share. The vulnerability of that moment became cathartic, connecting him to his present while allowing for the beauty of his past to mingle with it. Clara and the group listened intently, their presence wrapping him in a supportive embrace. "Your stories are important, Samuel," Clara said softly. "They remind us of how love transcends even the darkest times."

Their encouragement pierced through his heart like rays of sunshine breaking through heavy clouds, igniting within him a newfound understanding of love and loss. He realized that sharing these stories was not solely a reflection of his grief, but also a celebration of the life they could still honor. As the cycle of seasons progressed, so too did Samuel's relationship with grief. The once oppressive weight transformed into a bittersweet companion, allowing him to carry both sorrow and joy simultaneously. The chaos he faced became intertwined with the beauty of shared experiences and the warmth of love.

One winter afternoon, Samuel found himself walking through a park blanketed in snow, the world around him transformed into a shimmering white. The cold air invigorated him, and a sense of peace settled over his heart. During this solitary walk, he reflected on all that he had shared and how those connections had filled the void left by his loss. In that moment, as he marveled at the beauty of life, he encountered a young girl building a snowman nearby. A small group of her friends surrounded her, their laughter echoing through the crisp air. Seized by a momentary impulse, he approached them and offered to help. "Can I help you with that?" he asked, feeling a swell of nostalgia at the sight of their joy.

The little girl looked up at him, her eyes shining with excitement. "Can you make the snowman's face?" she asked, her delight infectious.

Samuel knelt down, engaging in the pure chaos of childhood joy. As they molded the snow, he found himself laughing freely, the sound blending harmoniously with the giggles of the children around him. It was a simple act, yet it brought a depth of warmth to his heart, a reminder that moments of connection could break through even the bleakest of days. When he finished the snowman and stepped back to admire their work, the children erupted into cheers, throwing snow into the air with childlike abandon. The energy surrounding him was electric, and he felt a stirring of joy that mingled seamlessly with his memories of childhood play. It was a moment that served as a reminder that life may present chaos, but within that disarray are beautiful moments that shimmer like jewels waiting to be discovered.

After that day, insights thrived within him like the resplendent blooms of spring. Samuel recognized that, while grief anchored him for a time, it did not imprison him. Instead, it unveiled a rich landscape of connection, joy, and shared humanity, guiding him through moments of laughter even amidst sorrow. As he continued to gather with Clara and the crew, he began to cultivate a small tradition of his own each month; they would volunteer to help those in need at a nearby shelter. At first, Samuel felt apprehensive about diving into this chaotic service space, but he soon understood that, amid all the unpredictability, kindness served as a balm for the soul. Together, they cooked meals, served food, and shared stories with the guests at the shelter, and in doing so, transformed their own chaos into acts of compassion. Each experience deepened the bonds among them, creating a familial embroidery woven with threads of love and understanding, a quaint harmony that contrasted the discord of their individual lives.

In these moments of giving back, Samuel found something profound; the realization that the chaos of life, while unsettling, became fertile ground for empathy and connection. Suddenly, the storm's roar didn't resonate so harshly. Rather, he began to view it through a different lens: an opportunity to forge connections that would help him navigate those tumultuous waters. As the sun began to set on a particularly chaotic month filled with more ups and downs than he could count, the group gathered again at the apartment. Clara stood before them, her presence anchoring the collective energy. "To chaos and the connections, we've found in it," she declared, raising her glass once more.

Acknowledging the essence woven into their journeys, each person offered their own versions of joy, laughter, and resilience, an attestation to their ability to rise amidst the chaos, embracing its complexity. The night unfolded into a joyous celebration, punctuated by heartfelt stories, shared laughter, and an appreciation for the delicate beauty found within disorder. Amidst the revelry, Samuel reflected on how far he had come; how, through chaos, he had discovered the heart of life nestled profoundly within human connection.

As the evening reached its peak, Samuel felt a deep sense of gratitude encompassing him. He turned to look at Clara, who had become a beacon of light through his darkest hours. The laughter that echoed around the room forged an indelible connection, precious and irreplaceable. In the midst of chaos, he had found strength, solace, and, above all, a reminder that joy could be found even in life's tumultuous moments. With every shared laugh, every heartfelt story, he understood that it was through unity and compassion that he could transcend the loneliness of loss, transforming grief into a tapestry rich with resilience, connection, and hope. Samuel raised his glass, joined by friends who had become like family. Their voices echoed joyfully around him, a symphony played in a world that was forever in motion, filled with chaos, yet vibrant with the threads of love that tied them together, illuminating their paths, lifting them from despair, and allowing them to dance amid the storms of life.

Lessons from the Storm

The cacophony of the storm rattled the windows, each crash of thunder reverberating through the house like a troubled heart. It felt as if the whole world outside had become a manifestation of chaos, with relentless rain pounding against the roof and wind howling like a chorus of spirits echoing its unsettled fury. Inside, however, the protagonist sat in a dimly lit room, cocooned in a quilt of thoughts that were both familiar and foreign. The violence of the storm outside was matched by an internal tempest of memories, emotions, and realizations that demanded to be unraveled. In moments like these, at the edge of emotional and physical chaos, the protagonist found themselves at a crossroads, a juncture where closure became an elusive whisper amidst the din.

The past few weeks had thrust tumult into their life with a ferocity they had never anticipated. Loss had settled heavily on their shoulders, unspoken grief hanging like damp fog around their being. Each day was marked by a surging tide of unprocessed feelings, the remnants of conversations left unfinished and questions that hung direly in the air. It was during such storms, both in nature and in the soul that one often glimpses a deeper truth, a lesson to be woven into the fabric of their life. Memories flooded into their mind, juxtaposing the most vibrant moments against the relentless backdrop of grief. They recalled the last time they had spoken to their loved one, laughter shared like warm sunlight cutting through dark clouds. They had talked about trivialities, like the weather, plans for the weekend, and the absurdity of life's sudden twists.

It was in those mundane details that real life often flourished, a criminally overlooked treasure that in retrospect shimmered with truth and beauty. Yet that warmth now feels tainted, a memory bittersweet. The wind howled fiercely, and for a brief moment, it sounded like the voice of their lost loved one, urging them to triumph over sorrow. The protagonist realized, with heavy clarity, that life itself is woven with shades of chaos, the unpredictability of existence manifesting in countless forms. It wasn't merely the storm outside that raged, but the unpredictable ebb and flow of life that continuously sculpted and reshaped one's innermost self.

Just as the current chaos eventually give way to calm, perhaps the same could be true for their soul's unrest. In the thick of grief, it is easy to feel isolated, as if the deluge of emotions swirls around you in layers that keep you from connecting to the outside world. Yet the protagonist understood that vulnerability, despite the heaviness and suffocation, was also liberating. Each breach of the dam led to moments where connection revived their spirit. Conversations with friends, consultations with a therapist, shared memories with family, these were not signals of weakness but rather beacons illuminating the path through the chaos, offering glimmers of closure entwined with love. The storm outside began to wane, the furious rain subsiding into a soft drizzle. As if nature were echoing the protagonist's own reflections, peace cradled the aftermath of chaos. With every crack of thunder ending and each gust of wind dying down to a gentle breeze, they felt a subtle shift within, a calm that began to replace the tempest. They had learned, through the flurry of tears and laughter, that acceptance often arrives dressed in vulnerability; grief and healing followed closely, like steadfast companions. They recalled the characteristically bright conversations that had echoed within walls now silent. In life, those moments often felt insignificant, fleeting brushstrokes on the canvas of existence. But in retrospect, they were colors that infused life with depth, shading the protagonist's world in ways they had previously failed to recognize.

The protagonist now had the insight to appreciate how each moment lived could enrich one's own tapestry of being, regardless of how chaotic life appeared in hindsight. Tenderly, they remembered the ways their loved one had navigated through life's storms. That person embraced uncertainty, often approaching challenges with a mischievous glimmer in their eye, inviting laughter even in the most trying of times. They exhibited a rare strength, an acceptance of life's unpredictability not as an enemy but as a dance partner. Each misstep, each moment of vulnerability enriches life's choreography, culminating in memories that would unfold across a lifetime. This newfound perspective was not easily attained; it was borne of the hard-earned lessons that come only from confronting grief in its rawest, most unfiltered form. It embodied the truth that from darkness, light could indeed emerge if one is willing to look for it. The chaotic moments in life possess a potent alchemy; they can catalyze transformation, guiding individuals to uncover strengths and grapple with the fear that comes with vulnerability.

As the storm continued to dissipate, they felt the symbolic layers of that turmoil peeling away. Each layer represented moments of isolation that had, for so long, felt impenetrable, a shield against the outside world built from sorrow and loss. By facing their grief head-on, they realized those walls were not entrenched barriers, but woven elements, integral to their own story. The confusion and the tumult were not adversaries, but rough stones shaping the pathway toward healing. In shared grief, the bonds of connection grew stronger, each thread delicately stitching together a narrative that transcended time and loss. They understood that every person carries a multitude of stories within a shade of grief and joy intertwined so intricately that to sever one without the other would be impossible. The protagonist expressed gratitude not only for their own lessons learned but also for the shared experiences of loss that strove for meaning amid chaos. Moreover, the protagonist began to recognize that it was in the act of embracing vulnerability reaching out, sharing stories, and allowing love in that genuine transformation manifested. They leaned into the idea that growth itself thrives in chaos, reshaping perspectives and encouraging souls to rise from the ashes.

This realization prompted the protagonist to reflect on their own reactions to discomfort; discomfort, too, was part of the human experience. The chaos of life was not merely a sequence of unfortunate events but a rich tapestry of experiences, interlaced with teachings waiting to be discovered. As they continued to reflect, a softness enveloped them, allowing them to integrate the fragments of their experiences into a holistic understanding of existence. They began to see each aspect of chaos not as a harbinger of doom but as a potential catalyst for positive change. For every dark moment, every tribulation weathered, an opportunity emerged inviting resilience to bloom from the seeds of pain. The protagonist understood that closure is not necessarily a neatly tied-up narrative; rather, it is the acknowledgement of chaos while allowing lessons to wash over you like gentle rain after a tempest. In embracing vulnerability, connections become tools for understanding the depths of both joy and sorrow. True closure, they realized, is the reconciliation that occurs when one learns from the storm and actively seeks to honor the memories that resonate within.

The storm waned to a silent mist, and the air felt fresher somehow, invigorated by the cleansing that had taken place. Rain could either drown you or nourish you; it depends on what perspective you choose to embrace. The protagonist sat up and gazed outside, the world seeming washed anew. Nature had its own way of renewing life and obliterating chaos, a subtle reminder that everything has its course, the tears shed could eventually seed a garden for tomorrow. Reflecting on the lessons from the storm, the protagonist felt a renewed sense of resolve. They began outlining practical pathways to continue integrating these revelations into their daily lives. Journaling became a retreat, allowing them to articulate thoughts and emotions that surged forth like a river unleashed after a long drought. They picked up their pen, letting the ink flow freely, crafting their narrative with each stroke, gaining clarity as the characters of their life's story emerged, each representing memories colored by love and sorrow.

In addition to writing, they sought to foster connections with others. They engaged in open dialogues, bereft of pretense and fragility. Reaching out, they spoke of their grief, invited vulnerability in conversations, and embraced shared narratives. They discovered that authentic relationships are nourished by transparency, and shared laughter mingled with tears became the threads that stitched their lives together once more. Each morning, the protagonist chose to seek the beauty life offered, despite the shadows that lingered. They simplified their lives, turning to nature and quiet moments for nourishment. A walk amidst the chirping birds and rustling leaves became a reminder of life's resilience; delicate blossoms emerging triumphantly after the most chaotic storms. They discovered within themselves a sense of purpose igniting anew, a mission to turn their loss into a catalyst for change, weaving their story with compassion and love. Closure would not come in a single moment of realization; it became a journey, an ongoing dialogue with loss.

The protagonist began to find peace in allowing the messiness of life to exist alongside the beauty they encountered. They learned that closure evolves into acceptance, which folds seamlessly into love, highlighting the intricate dance of grief and resilience. As the first rays of sunlight broke through the heavy clouds, the protagonist turned their gaze upward. A new day dawned, filled with possibility, an embodiment of those very lessons unearthed from chaos. They felt the warmth of hope settling in, igniting the spirit within, resolute and unwavering. The lessons from the storm had taught them that chaos cultivates resilience. Each tear shed, each moment of vulnerability embraced, was a step closer toward healing. Closure, they understood, is not an endpoint, but rather an evolving embrace of life's unpredictable beauty. As the protagonist prepared for the day ahead, filled with renewed purpose and compassion for themselves and others, they embraced the wisdom garnered from the storm. In its quiet aftermath, they found clarity, purpose, and an unwavering belief in the struggle toward luminosity forged in chaos.

The Language of Silence

Navigating Quiet Spaces

The air was thick with a soft tranquility as the protagonist stepped into the serene garden, an oasis removed from the chaos of daily life. Surrounded by lush greenery, the gentle rustle of leaves whispered melodies that echoed through time, each sound mingling with the tender sigh of the wind. This was a sacred space, a gallery of silence where thoughts and feelings could dance freely, unencumbered by the weight of spoken words. It was here, in this quiet sanctuary, that they would begin to unearth layers of emotion long buried beneath the surface.

As sunlight filtered through the branches overhead, casting dappled patterns on the ground, the protagonist felt an inexplicable connection to nature, to the very essence of life surrounding them. Each footfall seemed to reverberate through their soul, resonating with unvoiced sentiments and memories stifled by the noise of the outside world. Stepping further into the depths of the garden, they surrendered to the allure of silence, a blanket that wrapped around their heart and mind. The stillness enveloped them completely, and in this sacred quietude, the protagonist began to reflect on the nature of the bonds they held with those they loved. It struck them how often silence filled the spaces between conversations with family and friends. Those ineffable moments, rich with meaning, contrasted sharply with the distractions of everyday life. They realized how silence, too, could be a language, a profound way to connect without the need for words.

The protagonist paused beneath a large oak tree, its gnarled branches reaching outward like ancient arms ready to embrace the world. This tree seemed to hold a repository of untold stories, its very presence a testament to the passage of time and experience. Leaning against its sturdy trunk, they closed their eyes, allowing the serenity to seep into their bones. Memories flooded back, sparked by the subtle fragrances of damp earth and blooming jasmine. There were memories of lazy afternoons spent with a grandparent, sitting side by side in comfortable silence while watching the clouds drift lazily across the sky. What words had they exchanged? Hardly any, yet the bond forged in those moments felt stronger than any eloquent dialogue could provide. The weight of love was often carried in shared silence, in the way their hands would brush together, or the gentle nod of understanding that passed between them. It was as if the silence wrapped around the stories they hadn't spoken aloud, preserving them like delicate petals pressed between the pages of a cherished book.

Opening their eyes, the protagonist was struck by a vibrant patch of wildflowers nearby, their colors as vivid as the emotions they represented. Each bloom symbolized a range of feelings of joy, sorrow, nostalgia, and reminders of the shared moments that had shaped their life. They knelt to take a closer look, fingers tracing the fragile edges of the petals, marveling at how something so beautiful could arise from the quiet beneath.

It was at that moment that the protagonist recognized how often they had overlooked silence as a means of connection. They thought of their best friend, someone with whom laughter came easily, but who also sat alongside them during moments of deep heartache, days filled with melancholy when words failed. Sitting together in such profound silence, they had shared invisible burdens, their souls entwined in understanding without the need for affirmation.

The protagonist's thoughts drifted again, this time to a recent loss. A beloved family member had passed, and the absence felt palpable, vibrating in the silence of their home. How strange it was that in the wake of grief, it was the quiet hours that weighed heaviest, the moments when the absence of the deceased was felt most acutely. Mourning was never loud; it existed in the thrumming silence, in the empty chair at the dinner table, in the unmade bed that held faded memories. Here, in the garden, the layers of loss began to surface. Each inhalation carried the essence of those no longer present, and the protagonist struggled with the unexpressed emotions that danced just beneath their skin. They felt raw and exposed, as though the silence had drawn forth feelings desperate for acknowledgment.

The protagonist chose to lean further into that silence, hoping to uncover the emotions trapping them under the surface. It was both terrifying and liberating to sit with grief, to allow it to swell instead of fighting back against the tide. In this way, the silence became a cocoon, nurturing the fragile threads of unresolved feelings stretching toward the light. As they surrendered to the silence, the essence of life continued to pulse around them. A gentle breeze stirred the leaves, whispering softly to the flowers, creating a symphony that was both haunting and beautiful. Listening intently, the protagonist began to discern the nuances hidden within that silence, messages carried in the flutter of petals, the serenity of still waters, and the warmth of sunlight filtering through the branches. It was a reminder that although words may inform, silence can heal.

Absorbed in this moment, the protagonist's mind wandered to the unfulfilled conversations left hanging in the air, the unsaid words lingering like ghosts. How often had they refrained from expressing what mattered most? It became painfully clear that sometimes the most impactful expressions of love and grief resided in the spaces where syllables failed, in the hollow echoes of silence that rang truer than any heartfelt pronouncement. The protagonist allowed an emotion to surface, a well of tears filled their eyes. The garden, a witness to the complexities of their feelings, stood as a reminder of what it meant to live, love, and eventually lose. Among the wildflowers, the idea of vulnerability gave rise to a recognition that by embracing silence, they were also embracing their own fragility. This acknowledgment brought forth a sense of peace, one that sat heavily yet soothingly in their chest.

Gradually, as they sat there beneath the tree, waves of realization washed over them like the ebb and flow of the ocean. They began to understand that silence played an integral role in growth, that just as nature thrived in quietude, so too did the human heart. Just as the garden bloomed year after year, nourished by seasons both rich and barren, so too could they cultivate their feelings, allowing silence to nurture the roots of their emotional existence. The protagonist looked up at the vibrant canopy of leaves above. It was an ever-changing world, a reminder that nothing in life was fixed. The silence enveloping them transformed, becoming not a void but a vibrant shade of potential. They realized they could navigate their emotions like careful gardeners, tending to the memories of those they loved, cherishing the moments spent in silence, while nurturing the connections that would continue to grow.

And as their heart swelled with the recognition of their capacity for love and loss, they made a promise to themselves. The promise to honor the silences, to invite intimacy into those unspoken moments, and to find ways to articulate their feelings, not only for themselves but also on behalf of those they had lost. Because each moment spent in meaningful silence was an opportunity, a moment to deepen the bonds that transcended time, a chance to connect on a level that surpassed mere words. The realization was bittersweet but cathartic, providing a balm for the wounds they had so carefully tended. Instead of viewing silence as a chasm to be filled with empty chatter, they recognized it as a bridge, a way to reach deeper understanding, acceptance, and love. And even though the silence carried the weight of unfulfilled conversations, it also held the promise of new beginnings, of relationships that continued to evolve beyond the physical realm.

As dusk began to settle in, the soft hues of orange and pink painted the sky, a beautiful reminder of life's fleeting nature. The protagonist lingered in this sacred garden, allowing the quiet to become a constant companion. It was here that they recognized the profound depth of human experience, a testament to navigating the intricate spaces of love and loss, joy and sorrow.

With a heartwarming newfound resolution, they rose, brushing back the fallen leaves that had collected around them. As they took their leave of the garden, they understood that the language of silence would remain a deeply woven thread in their life narrative, an enduring bond that would continue to connect them to the past, the present, and the promise of tomorrow. Each step on the path back home became an affirmation of their journey, a tribute to all the moments shared and unshared, to the laughter, the tears, and the sacred silence that ensued. Silence, they saw, was not an abyss but a space rich with meaning, a precious thing to be cherished and honored. In navigating the quiet spaces, they had discovered a profound truth: that silence, rather than being an absence, was an integral part of existence, an eloquent companion in the exploration of love and connection that transcended time and space.

The Unsaid Bonds

The quiet settled around the protagonist like a warm blanket on a chilly night, wrapping them in a familiar cocoon that encouraged both reflection and introspection. Growing up in a home that valued the importance of silence, they often found themselves navigating between unspoken words and moments laden with heavy emotions. Silence had its own language, subtle, unassuming, a conversation that flowed in tandem with laughter, tears, and the unmeasurable weight of shared experiences.

One memory in particular swelled within them: a day when time seemed to stretch to accommodate the silence they shared with their grandfather on a fading autumn afternoon. The golden sun dipped low in the sky, casting long shadows across the lawn where the pair sat together in companionable stillness. Each sip of sweet tea, each rustle of leaves in the gentle breeze felt amplified, pregnant with meaning. The protagonist distinctly recalled the feeling of leaning back on the porch swing, the familiar creaking sound melding with the rustling whispers of the trees, a sound that echoed their hearts' tranquil expressions.

In that moment, no words were exchanged, yet an entire narrative unfolded. Grandfather's gaze, steady and knowing, reflected a lifetime of stories yet untold, years woven with laughter, hopes, and regrets. It was a silence that spoke louder than the mightiest of proclamations. As the sun began its descent, the protagonist felt an urge to break the serene stillness, to offer something, anything, to fill the space shared with their grandfather. Yet a profound understanding washed over them: sometimes the most meaningful exchanges occur in the void of silence, where feeling reigns supreme and words would only serve to fracture the delicate atmosphere they had constructed.

From that day on, the protagonist held this lesson close to their heart, recognizing that silence is not merely the absence of sound; it can also be a vessel of deep emotional connection, a way to convey empathy and understanding without uttering a single syllable. This realization began to shape their relationships as they moved through life, particularly during moments of loss and grief when language often falters beneath the weight of emotion.

As the years passed, similar moments of silence emerged, each one a poignant reflection of shared experiences interwoven with love and vulnerability. At family gatherings, there were times when laughter erupted around the dinner table, only to fall into a hushed reverence when the memory of lost loved ones seeped into the air like a thick fog. These moments, borne of sorrow yet tinged with warmth, allowed family members to exchange knowing glances, eyes radiating shared memories that filled the space between them. Here was where the magic of unspoken bonds thrived, each gaze a reminder of the strength found in togetherness.

During a particular holiday, while everyone took turns reminiscing about the jovial spirit of an aunt who had departed too soon, the protagonist found themselves enveloped in a comfortable silence after the stories came to an end. They and their cousins slowly gathered in the parlor around a flickering fireplace. The warmth emanating from the flames was a gentle shade of solace; the only sounds were the crackling of the fire and the soft ticking of the grandfather clock. In this serene environment, the protagonist felt a profound sense of belonging. Suddenly, the silent moments became a comforting balm for their hearts as they collectively mourned while celebrating the life and legacy of their beloved aunt.

These shared moments of silence often created an unbreakable bond, allowing family members to guide each other through their grief without the burden of articulating the exact depth of their pain. They felt tension dissolve into understanding, where no one had to bear the weight of emotions alone. It instilled a sense of unity, a reminder that in the tapestry of human connections, words were not always essential. As hands brushed against one another and fingers intertwined in solidarity, the protagonist knew that they were not just part of a dynamic conversation; they were participants in a sacred communion that embodied their shared history.

The protagonist began to observe this dynamic in friendships, too. They fondly recalled evenings sitting around a fire pit with friends while the stars blinked overhead, indifferent to the worries below.

When a friend's heart shattered after a painful breakup, there were no words to ease the sorrow, yet their presence was a steadfast pillar. The group would sit in silence, passing around a bottle of wine, sharing glances and subtle smiles, responding not with words but with touch, the warmth of a hand placed comfortingly on a knee, a gentle back rub, an understanding look. In those moments, the silence reframed their connection; words were unnecessary yet carried an immeasurable grace. Every heartbeat felt synchronized, every breath a testament to their camaraderie as it morphed into a powerful vehicle for nurturing their grief and love in balance.

The protagonist realized that silence, infused with empathy and understanding, became a space where healing could flourish, free from the limitations imposed by language. While grappling with loss, they understood that shared silence invited self-reflection in a way that words could not. It was a rare and intimate space, a contrast to the often-noisy world outside where everything clamored for attention. Here, their internal landscape could breathe.

In their quiet moments, the protagonist often found themselves reflecting on the intricate nature of relationships and how silence, often overlooked, could weave its fabric into the story of their lives. There were times they craved companionship but also needed the solace of silence, a balance that often eluded their more extroverted friends. Sitting together, the lack of chatter revealed deeper currents of understanding. They began to appreciate that even an uncomfortable silence could transition into something profound; while uncertainty hung in the air, it provided an opportunity for personal contemplation. This threshold of silence allowed them to uncover feelings oftentimes buried beneath layers of expectations and societal norms.

During the quiet, reflections flitted uneasily; thoughts bounced from memory to emotion, intertwined subtly in their consciousness. They often thought of the fleeting nature of life, how precious was this time spent not merely talking but simply being together. Those shared silences became markers in their imagination, leading them down memory lane where they explored uncharted territories of their grief. Whether it was concerning the loss of a parent, the estrangement from a sibling, or the simple longing for moments that could never be replicated, these thoughts found their way to the surface, spilling quietly into the shared silence that enveloped them.

As relationships evolved, grew deeper, or even faded, the protagonist learned to treasure those moments of silence. They would often find a seat beside their mother on a quiet evening, their shoulders grazing as they began to sip tea while taking in the twilight sky unfurling above. The older woman's wisdom emanated through the shared quiet; there was a familiarity in their silence, one that transcended the need for small talk. It was in the tranquility that the protagonist felt most connected to her, both understanding the weight of past losses and the shared grief they bore. Each white space became a canvas painted with emotion, colors blending softly as stories echoed throughout the years, unhurried by the rush of daily life. In these moments, their unspoken words conveyed a myriad of emotions: grief, relief, and acceptance. Words failed, yet hearts opened wide, breathing into the depths of love and remembrance.

At times, the protagonist felt overwhelmed by the enormity of emotions that silence could evoke. It was in those quiet hours that they realized how unexpressed sentiments could weigh heavy on one's heart. Occasionally, they faced the challenge of reconciling their own feelings with their loved ones', often unsure how to begin or how to bridge an ever-growing distance marked by silence. The pull to protect others from pain often kept them trapped in a cycle of unspoken worry, as one didn't want their emotional turmoil to disrupt the tenuous peace they shared.

Yet, as they continued to navigate this path, the protagonist saw beyond fear; they understood that silence could also gift them time to remain vulnerable. It imbued their relationships with a rich depth that could withstand the pressures of daily life, chronicling their own emotional journey along the way. They began to realize that sometimes the unsaid bonds offered the greatest value. Collective silences allowed everyone to touch the essence of each other's spirits without the potential distortions caused by harsh words. In shared silence, there was rhythmic beauty in unexpressed love, compassion that bridged the divides created by human imperfections.

In the end, the protagonist's understanding of silence deepened as life continued to weave its inexorable fabric of connections. Crossroads arose as friends that once sat together around starry skies distanced, shadows quietly absorbing them into their new realities. Characteristically, silence enfolded them as each transitioned into different phases of life, leaving behind the familiar companionship that had served as their sanctuary. Yet even amidst this change, they learned that the remnants of those shared moments would endure if there was something indelible about those silences, lingering long after voices faded into whispers.

They began to cherish the silence drawn from memory, acknowledging the unbreakable bond woven through heartbeats and shared breaths. Looking back at their relationships provided clarity about the essence of connection, how it flourished even when distance prevailed, only to be ignited anew with every ritual of remembrance. Years later, as the protagonist embarked on their journey of life anew, they realized that the powers of silence had infused unexpected beauty into their human experience, crafting a rich tapestry into which grief and love could merge as one.

The embrace of silence underlined the depth of each connection, capturing threads of intimacy that had intertwined lives, each emotionally reverberating through the timeless corridors of memory. In that simple understanding, silent or otherwise, the protagonist found their way through an ethereal dance entwining individual struggles and collective joys, resolved that love possesses its voice even in the absence of words. They embraced the journey ahead, forever grateful for the unsaid bonds, tenderly cradled in the embrace of silence, woven into the unfolding narrative of human existence.

Communicating Through Presence

The air was thick with stories left unspoken as the protagonist found themselves sitting in the quiet confines of a sun-drenched room. The soft light filtered through the sheer curtains, casting gentle patterns on the wooden floor. Outside, the world bustled with noise, a cacophony of laughter, chatter, and the rumble of cars that formed a stark contrast to the stillness enveloping them. In this sanctuary of silence, they became acutely aware of their surroundings, attuned to each subtle sound: the faint rustle of leaves outside, the distant chirping of birds, and the quiet heartbeat of their own life rhythm.

In this moment, the protagonist was not alone. Across from them sat an old friend, a familiar face marked by time and experience. Though no words were exchanged, an unspoken understanding flowed between them, deepening with every breath. They shared a space that transcended the limitations of language, a communion of souls that spoke volumes without uttering a single word.

The protagonist's mind wandered as they observed their friend. They noticed the slight furrow of concern on their brow, the way their hands rested on their knees, fingers intertwined like branches of ancient trees seeking support. The room absorbed their presence, wrapping them in an intimacy forged through years of shared memories, laughter, and silence. Each heartbeat resonated with unexpressed emotions, surging through the quiet like waves against the shore.

As memories stirred within them, the protagonist recalled moments when conversations had flowed freely, laughter erupting like fireworks. Yet there were also times when silence had enveloped them, thick and comforting, like a warm blanket on a chilly evening. Those silent exchanges were laden with significance, punctuated by shared glances, gentle nods, and heartfelt sighs. It became clear that silence, far from being merely an absence of sound, was a language of its own, a means of communicating emotions that words often failed to capture.

The protagonist settled deeper into their thoughts, reflecting on how often they had taken the comfort of silence for granted. They remembered evenings spent with family members, where rather than filling the air with chatter, they each found fulfillment in the shared space, muttering quietly as they read, the crackling of a fire in the hearth, or the occasional clink of cups as tea was served. Those moments held layers of connection that no exchange of words could replicate.

Silence had a way of peeling back the layers of their hearts, revealing vulnerabilities that might remain hidden behind the barricade of words. The protagonist marveled at how they could pour their heart into silence, and their friend would understand intuitively. It was a recognition of grief, of hope, of dreams yet to be realized. By simply being there, they offered each other a balm for the wounds that life had inflicted.

Their thoughts drifted to those who had come and gone from their lives, spirits now residing in memories. With each flicker of daylight that danced through the room, the protagonist felt the presence of lost loved ones. They remembered them vividly, each smile and touch lingering in the air like a haunting melody. Perhaps this was the weight of connection, the truth that love never truly vanished; it merely adapted, transformed into a resonance felt even in their absence.

In this embrace of quietude, the protagonist found themselves contemplating the essence of presence. What does it mean to truly share space with another? They considered the layers of meaning that lay beneath mere physical proximity. It was about being present, mindfully engaged in that moment, even when words became unnecessary. To share laughter, a tear, or even a sigh in silence was to enter a sacred realm of understanding.

The protagonist glanced at their friend. The depth of the relationship was palpable, radiating quietly like the waning light of the afternoon sun. They could feel the currents of their histories washing over them, each memory a thread binding them together. This awareness cemented a connection that resonated beyond life's fluid, transitory nature. Here, they were rooted in the present, navigating the silent waves that ebbed and flowed, a testimony to resilience and camaraderie.

Time slipped away, and as the sun began its descent, bathing the room in a warm golden glow, the protagonist felt a sense of awakening. In this space of tranquility, they discovered that silence offered a bridge to deeper intimacy. They realized that within these quiet moments, they had come to understand not just their friend but themselves as well, every unuttered regret, longing, and hope surfacing like delicate petals in a blooming garden.

They formed a mental tapestry, weaving images of treasured memories together into a vivid collage that would never fade, even in silence. Vibrant colors emerged, evoking laughter shared over late-night talks, whispers exchanged under the stars, and even the heavier hues of sorrow during farewells that had left lasting imprints on their hearts. Each elicited questions that hung unspoken in the air, circling like birds, waiting for the right moment to land.

In those moments, it went beyond mere cohabitation of a physical space; it grew into a commitment of emotional presence. The protagonist understood that the silence surrounding them was not an emptiness waiting to be filled but rather a rich landscape where thoughts could roam free. They could venture into the corners of their minds without fear, supported by the weight of quiet companionship.

With newfound clarity, they acknowledged the layers of their relationship with their friend. The protagonist intuitively sensed the threads that wove their lives together. Each laugh shared had sown seeds of trust, while every moment of grief became a powerful reminder that they were not alone. Together, they had navigated through storms, accompanied one another through darkness, and celebrated the dawn of new beginnings.

During these shared silences, every emotion was palpable, grief, nostalgia, joy, a spectrum painted across their faces in colors vibrant and deep. Within these fleeting moments, they had become storytellers of a different kind, narrators of their lives through gestures and glances. Each pulse of silence became a canvas, inviting them to etch their emotions in ways words might never achieve.

The protagonist drew in a breath, inhaling the delicately woven atmospheres of memory that flooded the room, sharpening their senses. They shut their eyes, enabling an inner vision unshackled from the mundane, a vivid tapestry of moments bright and beautiful. They painted pictures in their mind of everyone they missed, alive in their memories. And there it was: the sweet sound of remembrance mingled with the silence, a symphony played in the heart, murmuring softly through tender recollections.

They were grateful for the stillness that enveloped them, providing a safe harbor to navigate the labyrinth that was grief. In their hearts, they recognized that presence was not merely about physical proximity but the warmth of understanding that transcended everything.

As the evening light began to fade, the protagonist felt the need for new horizons. They longed to deepen connections forged in silence, to explore how these threads of shared companionship could stretch into the wider world. Inspired, they thought of embracing silence with others, seeking to quiet the noise that often drowned out deeper connections.

Imagine gathering friends not for conversation but to simply sit together beneath a canopy of stars, allowing the night to envelop them, sharing unspoken thoughts through the soft rustle of trees. They envisioned spaces created to honor that marvelous continuity etched into the fabric of shared experiences, where one could witness a simple presence dissolve the tension of a hard day.

As the protagonist sat across from their friend, an unassuming resolve solidified within them. They understood that life's deepest bonds often thrived in silence. Where words might have faltered, love persisted unscathed, illuminating the spaces left behind. And so, they made a vow to cherish those silent moments, to reach out with presence and embrace those who illuminated the shadows.

As the room began to darken with the fading light, the protagonist felt an ethereal energy surround them, an electric vibrancy that comes when souls resonate in harmony. Through this realization, they birthed an idea: to organize gatherings not structured by dialogue but rather inspired by the power of being together in quietude. They envisioned a movement, a series of evenings dedicated to the art of silent companionship, where participants could immerse themselves freely in one another's presence, honoring the beauty of shared stillness.

This was not merely a reaction to grief but an acknowledgment of the fragile threads that wove through relationships of loss, love, laughter, and everything in between. They understood now that often, the moments that left the strongest imprint were those that danced in silence, binding them together in a collective embrace of shared human experience.

As the protagonist sat with their friend, the fabric of their connection grew denser, spun from threads of kinship that would weather time. They resolved to honor this powerful presence, celebrating the connections that blossomed in quietude. The significance of presence shimmered before them, radiating warmth and solace. Broken or unbroken, the bonds of love bound them, and only in silence could they truly resonate.

With a silent vow echoing in their heart, the protagonist took in the warmth of companionship that filled the room. They understood that when the world became overwhelming, when life turned unbearably noisy, true solace often lay within the embrace of shared silence.

They rose to leave with a lingering peace, cradling the essence of presence that had burgeoned during that quiet time. As they stepped outside, the stars blinked high above, and the soft hum of the universe echoed in their ears. The protagonist felt the rich layers of their journey intertwine, nudging them forward into the great unknown, each memory, each moment of silence helping them navigate through life's uncertainties.

The connections cultivated in that serene oasis would linger in the corners of their mind, a reminder that amid loss and grief, there would always be space for love to flourish, even in silence.

Existential Threads

Tapestries of Connection

In the quiet moments between breaths, there lies an embroidery, one woven from the threads of lives intersecting, crossing paths in the most unexpected of ways. The protagonist stood in a sun-drenched park, the soft rustle of leaves above hinting at stories long forgotten and memories quietly waiting to be unveiled. Each whisper of the wind through the branches felt like the gentle tug of fate, urging them to reflect on the myriad connections that had shaped their life thus far.

The park was filled with families enjoying the golden afternoon, couples strolling hand-in-hand, and children's laughter ringing out like music. A small pond glimmered in the distance, where ducks paddled lazily, oblivious to the intricacies of the human experience unraveling around them. It was here, amidst the ordinary hustle of life, that the protagonist felt the weight of each transient interaction.

As they wandered along the winding path, each person they encountered seemed to represent a thread within this vast needlepoint, some strong and vibrant, others frayed and fading, yet all significant in their own right. The image of a drapery began to take shape in their mind, a vivid collage of color and texture that narrated the complexity of the human experience.

The first thread they pondered was that of an elderly man sitting on a weathered bench, his hands gripping a cane as he watched the world with a gentle smile. Every day, he reserved this spot, holding court with the invisible audience of passersby. This man, with his stories and quiet wisdom, had unknowingly imparted lessons to countless strangers. His nods and greetings were like markers on a map, chronicling the lives he touched, the moments shared, a hand waved, a smile exchanged.

Nearby, two teenagers were engrossed in animated chatter, their laughter rising above the ambient noise like the songs of birds. The protagonist marveled at the ease with which these young souls connected, their excitement and dreams intertwining, forging a bond that would someday be a cherished strand within their personal tapestries. Even fleeting interactions held meaning, as they were an exploration of identity yet to be determined by the paths they would choose.

Then there were the parents, navigating life with their young children. Every tickle, every word of encouragement was another thread sewn into their family's fabric. These moments were not just about nurturing the next generation; they were connections that would eventually ripple outward, influencing the children's relationships and experiences in ways unseen but profoundly impactful. The protagonist watched as a mother reassured her daughter, a gentle embrace wrapping around them like a protective layer, a thread of love promised to last despite the inevitable changes of time.

Reflecting on their childhood, the protagonist could recall

moments like these, candid exchanges with neighbors, a kind word from a teacher, laughter shared with friends. Each encounter had shaped their understanding of the world, contributing to the identity they carried. They had often taken these interactions for granted, viewing them as mere coincidences, unaware of the intricate designs forming in the backdrop of their lives.

The protagonist paused in front of a small art installation, its vibrant colors radiating joy. It showcased a tapestry of handwoven pieces contributed by the community, each square telling a unique story, an act of love, remembrance, a moment of triumph. The stories represented within the tapestry reflected shared grief, joy, and celebration, offering glimpses into the fragile threads of humanity.

As they studied the installation, the protagonist felt the connection to those anonymous creators resonating deep within them. The patterns they observed spoke volumes, the way blues intertwined with oranges, how dark threads met with sparkling strands to illuminate the contrast of human emotions. It was clear that these shared human experiences, both light and dark, intricately wove the fabric of existence, echoing the multitude of lives interspersed throughout time.

A child approached, tugging at their parent's sleeve. She pointed at a square depicting a sunflower, her eyes wide with wonder. "Mommy, look! It's beautiful!" The response was immediate, a radiant smile exchanged between mother and daughter, reminding them of the bond they had solidified through appreciation. In that simple moment, their expressions embodied the depth of connection, illustrating how joy can be found in the shared act of creation.

Turning their gaze from the art to the pond, the protagonist witnessed the ducks quarrel over breadcrumbs thrown by delighted children. Each peck and splash brought forth laughter and giggles, a ripple in the vast tapestry of life echoing the many interactions taking place. How curious it was that these simple creatures were also part of this grand design, their lessons of abundance and competition mirroring those of humanity.

Walking along the water's edge, the protagonist considered the nuances woven in and out through the years, those seemingly insignificant moments replaying like a montage. They remembered a brief taxi ride on a rainy day, sharing small talk with the driver who spoke of his dreams of becoming an artist. How gentle connections can turn two strangers into fellow travelers on the journey of life.

Even disruptions they mused held significance. An argument with a friend that brought them closer, the grief shared in the wake of a shared loss, or the silence that sometimes follows a betrayal, all these elements contributed to the thread of a life lived. Each story mattered. Each connection mattered. Every moment was an opportunity to forge another thread within the canvas of existence.

During their time in high school, the protagonist once sat next to a girl in class who always doodled the most beautiful spirals in her notebooks. Through fleeting eye contact, silent glances turned into unspoken camaraderie, their shared passion for art intertwined. Years later, they would cross paths again, each becoming a successful artist, carrying within them the energy of that initial spark ignited in shared solitude.

The protagonist wondered how many times those interwoven moments would reflect in a larger narrative. As they gazed upon the collective lives blossoming around them, the realization struck: no relationship, no matter how minuscule, could be dismissed. Each one contributed to a storyline that extended beyond the immediate, casting wide ripples that influenced future generations.

A couple walked by their hands laced together, an unspoken dialogue shared through gentle squeezing. The essence of love, the golden thread, connects these souls upon a journey filled with anticipation. Unrecognized by them, they were crafting a legacy of connection that would weave into the hearts of others, a blend of hope and warmth that would generate endless echoes in a world where love remains a beacon.

As the sun began to dip lower in the sky, casting long shadows that danced along the path, the protagonist felt the weight of reflection settle upon them. They recalled their late grandmother, who had always said that life is woven from chance and choice. It resonated deeply now, how choices to connect, moments of vulnerability, and the courage to reach out to one another create the fabric through which our lives run.

Stepping into the quiet of the surrounding trees, they felt increasingly aware of the connections beneath the surface, the ones, like the gnarled roots of ancient trees, intertwining underground, hidden from view yet crucial for survival. These connections fostered resilience and strength; they anchored the individual strands as they weathered the test of time.

It was this understanding that brought a sense of peace to the protagonist's heart. In recognizing the unseen tapestry, they could let go of past grievances and embrace hope, a realization that apologies could be exchanged, hearts could be mended, and new connections could bloom. The multicolored threads shone brighter against the backdrop of a shared narrative, a reminder that life, much like a tapestry, continues to unfold.

Each thread was a testament to possibilities yet to be explored, moments yet to be shared. The protagonist envisioned future encounters, where unknown connections awaited just around the corner: a fellow traveler on a train, a stranger offering help in an unexpected moment, or a mentor providing guidance during tough times. These new threads had yet to come into existence but would shape the protagonist's life in ways yet unrealized.

Leaving the park, the protagonist recognized that they held the power to add new patterns to the embroidery they carried, every little action, kindness, and gesture knit together in celebration of shared humanity. The thought warmed their spirit, filling them with anticipation for chapters yet to unfold.

Returning home, they glimpsed life anew, aware of how weaving in love, gratitude, and compassion could enrich their experiences. They picked up a paintbrush, envisioning their next creation as an homage to the tapestry of connection that bound humanity, a canvas celebrating moments shared. Each stroke was a reminder that existence is intricately woven, reminding them that in the end, it is the bonds we create and nurture that define our lives.

As dusk settled around them, the fading light invited the universe to cloak the world in silence. They felt an embrace from the inner tapestry that continued to tie them to everyone who had walked beside them, molding their identity with the stories left behind. The protagonist knew their journey was only just beginning; the threads they would encounter in the future would lead them to vibrant new patterns. They would continue to stitch together stories that illustrated the beauty of existence.

With every step, they vowed to intertwine the delicate strands of connections, painting a breathtaking mural of life, love, and the unbreakable bonds of humanity.

Unity Amidst Diversity

The sun dipped behind the horizon, painting the sky with strokes of orange and pink, as the protagonist meandered through the bustling streets of the city. Each step echoed with the rhythm of diverse lives, punctuated by snippets of laughter, fragments of conversation, and the soft hum of different cultures blending harmoniously. It was an ordinary day, yet the air felt charged with potential for connection, like an invisible thread weaving through the fabric of existence.

As the protagonist navigated through the crowd, their eyes fell upon a small park nestled between towering buildings, a pocket of tranquility amidst the urban chaos. Drawn by an instinctive pull, they stepped into the park, which felt like a world apart, a microcosm brimming with vibrant life. Here, people from various backgrounds gathered, each carrying stories that formed an intricate tapestry of humanity.

An elderly man sat on a bench, his weathered face a map of enduring experiences. He was feeding the pigeons, scattering breadcrumbs with gentle precision. The protagonist approached him, curiosity ignited.

"Excuse me," they said, taking a seat beside him. "What brings you here today?"

The man looked up, his eyes sparkling with a hint of nostalgia. "This place reminds me of my childhood in Italy. I came here every day after school," he began, his accent lacing the air with warmth. "We'd feed the birds and share stories. The world was different then, but the essence of connection was the same."

As he spoke, the protagonist felt an electric shock of empathy. His childhood memories were not merely echoes of the past; they danced in tandem with their own experiences of playfulness, innocence, and the universal language of laughter. They quickly understood that despite the vast ocean of time and distance that separated their lives, the bond of memory tied them together in the present.

"Do you miss it?" the protagonist asked, a sympathetic tone coloring their voice.

"Every day," he admitted. "But I also find joy in the present. Stories are meant to be shared, and every new encounter creates a new thread in our tapestry."

The protagonist pondered his words, realizing that life is much like a tapestry, where each thread represents a unique experience. It dawned on them that our differences, rather than barriers, are the very fabric of human connection. Inspired, they thanked him for sharing and continued their stroll through the park, letting the ebb and flow of life surround them.

Not far away, they spotted a young mother with her child, who was intently focused on a project of his own: a hand-drawn picture of a colorful world. The protagonist watched as he carefully chose crayons, his small fingers dancing over the paper, creating vibrant images of a fantastical realm.

"Hey there," the protagonist said, kneeling to get a closer look. "What are you creating?"

"A world where everyone is friends and we all help each other," the boy replied, an earnestness in his voice that struck a chord in the protagonist's heart.

"That sounds like a beautiful world," they said, genuinely impressed. "What else happens in your world?"

"We play! And we have food from everywhere! Like pizza from Italy and tacos from Mexico!" he proclaimed, his eyes wide with excitement.

Here was a child, unburdened by prejudice, already recognizing the strength in diversity long before the world would attempt to confine his understanding. The protagonist felt a swell of hope, realizing that this innocence carried the potential for unity, a reminder that even within their differences lay common threads of friendship and love.

"Why do you think it's important for everyone to be friends?" the protagonist asked, intrigued by the child's insights.

"Because together we make everything better! If we share our stories and food, we can all feel happy!"

The boy's fervor radiated positivity, and the protagonist couldn't help but smile. As they continued their conversation, the memory of their own childhood surfaced, the naïve, untarnished belief that connection was natural, effortless, and essential. They exchanged contact information with the mother, wishing to keep in touch, and, for a fleeting moment, they felt the warmth of interconnectedness envelop them like a comforting embrace.

Further along the path, the protagonist encountered a small gathering of people from different ethnicities, seated in a circle on the grass. The rhythmic sound of drums resonated in the air, accompanied by melodious voices harmonizing in a language that felt both foreign and familiar. Drawn in by the infectious energy, the protagonist approached and was welcomed warmly.

"Join us! We're sharing stories from our homelands through music." A young woman with a radiant smile extended an invitation, her hands outstretched toward the protagonist.

As they settled down, the group shared their roots, each person recounting how their background influenced their current journey. The Nigerian artist spoke passionately of his heritage's rich storytelling traditions, emphasizing the importance of oral history in preserving their culture.

"In our stories, we find wisdom from our ancestors," he explained, his voice filled with reverence. "They teach us about our identity and remind us of the struggles that shaped our communities."

His words resonated deeply within the protagonist, who recognized similar threads woven through their own family's narrative. They thought of the stories passed down through generations, tales of resilience and love that reflected triumphs and tribulations.

Another voice broke through, this time, a woman from Syria shared her experiences of fleeing her homeland, recounting the bittersweet journey of finding home in a foreign land. Her strength shone even through the sorrow that lingered in her story.

"Diversity is what drives us to survive," she said, her eyes reflecting a depth of understanding that traversed pain. "We honor those who cannot speak by sharing our stories. In each other's narratives, we find pieces of ourselves, and that nurtures unity amidst our differences."

The protagonist could feel the weight of each story reverberate within them, the collective power of shared experiences forming a powerful bond. It was a confirmation of what they were beginning to understand: every anecdote, every life shaped by diverse experiences, enriches the whole.

As the sun dipped lower, casting golden hues across the group's gathering, the protagonist underscored a crucial aspect: how the tales shared not only conveyed personal struggles but also illuminated paths toward understanding and empathy. The forced divisions of race, culture, and background began to dissolve as they reveled in their common humanity.

"Despite where we come from, we all seek love, security, and understanding," another participant chimed in, capturing the essence of belonging. "It's recognizing these commonalities that tether us."

As night fell, the gathering morphed into a celebration of love, rhythm, and storytelling, where the protagonist found solace and strength. They realized that the intricate tapestry these people wove with their lives was a testament to resilience, highlighting the beauty found within differences rather than the discomfort it often generates.

From this newfound realization, the protagonist decided they were not merely an observer of life's richness; they sought to live it. Armed with the understanding that their own story intertwined with the myriad tales encountered that evening, they left the park transformed, each memory, each encounter creating a new thread connecting them to the greater fabric of existence.

Days passed, and life continued to unfold. The protagonist's heart remained tethered to that park, the memories they had gathered pressing gently against their consciousness. An idea blossomed, a desire to delve deeper into the lives surrounding them.

Over the next week, they initiated conversations with coworkers, neighbors, and even strangers met on public transportation. Each interaction yielded the sharing of stories; laughter and tears erupted as anecdotes flowed freely. An immigrant's tale of leaving everything behind amid political chaos, an artist's passion for painting cultural landscapes, and a teacher's struggle to bridge gaps in understanding.

The protagonist began to see threads materializing before them, fragile yet powerful connections binding lives in ways previously obscured beneath the weight of superficial judgments. Their heart swelled with appreciation; the world felt alive with possibility.

One afternoon, under the sprawling branches of a familiar oak tree in the park, they organized a gathering, a potluck of sorts, inviting people from their neighborhood, each encouraged to share a dish and a story representative of their backgrounds. The vibrant aroma of spices filled the air as everyone arrived, each carrying a piece of home that spoke to their identity.

The event unfolded as a joyous celebration, laughter ringing through the leaves above. Stories were exchanged alongside every course, and the protagonist felt a warmth and belonging unlike ever before. Shared meals led to shared experiences, and the walls that once divided them crumbled under the weight of kinship and understanding.

As the sun dipped below the horizon, casting a golden glow, the gathering transformed. People began to dance, the blend of music articulating the unspoken emotions woven into the fabric of their lives, happiness, sorrow, hope, and remembrance. It was in that moment that the protagonist saw the embodiment of their revelation: unity amidst diversity.

The bliss in the air was palpable, a collective acknowledgment that every voice, every experience enriched their existence. They understood now that life's richness is amplified when we embrace our diversity, for it is that very variation that colors our world in breathtaking hues.

Through powerful anecdotes and shared memories, the protagonist had unearthed a profound truth, that they are not isolated threads, but rather integral to an expansive tapestry woven across time and space, where each difference serves not to divide but to unite in the shared human experience that withstands the test of time.

In that moment, as laughter and music harmonized under the night sky, they felt the threads of humanity intertwining, life's complex and beautiful quilt, emblematic of hope and connection, alive in the unfolding stories waiting to be discovered.

The Strength of Shared Stories

The warmth of the fireplace crackled softly in the dim light of the living room, casting gentle shadows on the walls. Gathered around a large wooden table were family members, their faces lit with anticipation. It was a gathering that had taken place every year since the passing of the matriarch, each person carrying their own memories and stories made poignant by the absence that echoed in the room. The protagonist sat among them, feeling an almost palpable sense of connection, a tapestry woven of shared histories and experiences.

In this sacred space, the air was thick with the fragrance of cinnamon and fresh-baked bread, the sounds of gentle laughter and quiet reminiscing accompanying the atmosphere. It was a mixture of joy and sorrow that enveloped them, a celebration of the lives that had come before and the stories that shaped their present being. The protagonist could feel the weight of their ancestors in the stories that lingered in the air, voices that had faded with time yet remained alive in the memories of those present.

As the protagonist's grandmother began to speak, the warm, raspy tones of her voice pulled everyone's attention, and the room quieted in reverence. "I remember the night your grandfather brought home the first Christmas tree, full of hope and anticipation. He spent hours embellishing it with paper ornaments we crafted together, laughter filling the house as we searched for the perfect spot to place the star on top." She smiled softly, her eyes shimmering with fond memories.

The protagonist listened intently, leaning in closer. Each story held within it the essence of what it meant to be part of this family, a narrative that transcended time. This particular tale not only painted a vivid picture of love and joy but also served as a reminder that memories are the threads stitching people together, sometimes vibrant with laughter, sometimes shadowed by loss, yet always binding.

As more stories spilled forth, the protagonist marveled at how this simple act of sharing connected them all. One by one, family members contributed stories passed down through generations: tales of courage, hardship, resilience, and hope. Each narrative wove new patterns into the existing fabric of their family history, connecting the present with the distant past.

The protagonist found themselves reflecting on the significance of these shared stories, the way each anecdote barely touched the surface of the person from whom it originated. It dawned on them that these narratives were not merely recollections; they were legacies steeped in emotions, teaching moments that carried lifetimes of experiences.

It was not just the tales of triumph and success that resonated; it was also the stories of struggle, those raw, unfiltered accounts of days when hope seemed lost. It was then that the protagonist began to see how these memories formed a common thread, visible yet intangible, linking them to their ancestors, grounding them in legacy.

They could hear Uncle James retelling his childhood adventure of escaping a particularly sticky situation with a mischievous raccoon, which had rummaged through the family picnic basket. Everyone laughed, but as they did, the protagonist recognized a deeper connection, the vibrancy of life captured in the cherished moments of mischief. It highlighted how light could flicker in the darkest of times, a testament to resilience and laughter amidst chaos.

As the stories continued, the protagonist noticed something transformative happening within them. It felt as though the stories were merging not only with the shared past but also intertwining with their own narrative, inviting them to contribute their unique threads. It was an awakening to the importance of storytelling, how each person's voice could enrich the collective tapestry of existence.

With a courageous breath, the protagonist decided to share a story of their own, a moment etched in memory from their early years, an incident that had shaped them in ways they had not fully appreciated until now. They spoke of the summer spent with their grandfather in the countryside, planting seeds in the garden, mirroring the resilience found in the family's stories. "He often said that every flower had its story, just like every person. Some bloom quickly, others take time, but each one of them matters. Just like us."

As they spoke, the faces around the table lit up with empathy and understanding, the room feeling even cozier than before. In that instance, the protagonist felt the building bonds transform into a quilt of warmth, each thread representing a unique story yet contributing to a larger narrative.

It was a moment of pure connection where the protagonist understood the beauty of shared stories, their power to heal, inspire, and motivate. They realized that the very act of storytelling forged pathways to understanding among individuals, bridging gaps that often seemed insurmountable. As the tales unfolded, they encouraged vulnerability and openness, allowing pain and joy to coexist.

The protagonist saw it clearly: this was the essence of humanity intertwined through stories, embracing imperfections, acknowledging burdens, and celebrating transformations.

As the evening progressed, the protagonist felt the pressure of generational expectations lift slightly, recognizing that each shared story held the promise of vulnerability and connection. With each retelling, there was an opportunity for growth, a space to revisit lost moments or celebrate life anew. They reflected on how stories had been shared for centuries, threading the past with the present while inviting glimpses of the future.

Though their voices were not physically present in the room, the essence of generations coursed around them like a gentle breeze. With each story entrusted to the next, the protagonist's sense of belonging strengthened. They understood that in recognizing and embracing the narratives within their lineage, they were also acknowledging themselves, their hopes, fears, and dreams resonating with the rhythm of those who came before.

The conversations flowed, unhurried and rich, and as the night deepened, so too did the understanding of how legacies are built. The protagonist began to appreciate the threads of influence that connected them to their ancestors, each story another stitch in the vast fabric of existence. In these moments, it was clear that they were not just listening; they were becoming participants in a dialogue that transcended time and space.

They could feel the weight of responsibility settle upon their shoulders, a gentle reminder that they, too, were now weavers of this tapestry, entrusted to carry forward the legacies shared through storytelling.

As the clock chimed at the late hour, the table was adorned with remnants of food and shared laughter. Perspectives shifted, and the protagonist felt the urge to preserve these emotions, to nurture the stories they had heard. Their heart brimmed with gratitude, not just for the tales but for being a conduit of collective memory.

Outside the window, shadows lengthened under the moonlight, and the protagonist sat back, embracing a quiet moment of reflection.

They felt an undeniable urge to connect these stories with the world, eager to weave their own threads into the larger human tapestry. They realized that these narratives, rich with experiences, could transcend their living room, spilling over into communities, binding strangers through shared experiences and struggles.

It became increasingly clear to the protagonist that everyone holds the potential to contribute to a narrative broader than their individual lives. Each voice, each experience, adds depth and richness to our shared humanity, a legacy that spans generations and encourages growth even beyond physical absence. In essence, these stories are the heartbeats of the human experience.

The revelation washed over them like a gentle tide, and a resolve began to solidify: the stories they had inherited would not dim or fade but would be spoken, written, and celebrated. From now on, the protagonist vowed to honor this legacy, to remember that every person they met, every encounter, held significance and potential. The act of sharing stories belonged to everyone, an invitation to forge connections that could inspire and heal.

As they drew closer to the heart of their intended journey, the protagonist knew they would carry this wisdom with them, the responsibility to acknowledge every voice that has and would ever flow into the currents of life. It was a journey of exploration, to find stories that resonate and ripple outward, inviting others to remember their own connections to the human tapestry.

They understood that the essence of these stories could nurture empathy, helping those around them bridge differences, dissolve barriers of judgment, and realize the fundamental truth of shared existence: we are all but threads in an intricate design.

In that realization, the protagonist began envisioning a future filled with gatherings that not only celebrate but also inspire the sharing of stories among diverse voices, emphasizing the enriching experience of stepping into someone else's narrative. They thought of ways to create space for dialogue in their community, open forums, storytelling evenings, and online platforms where these memories could be shared freely and joyously.

The imagery of a vibrant tapestry remained imprinted on their mind, represented by the lives that had woven it together. Discovering newfound empowerment, they no longer viewed their stories as solitary but as part of a greater whole. The blending of experiences urged the protagonist to step into a space where they could foster collective growth with the threads of shared narratives.

It would illuminate a path forward, not solely for them but for everyone who encounters the stories waiting to be told.

As the night settled into silence, the protagonist gazed at the darkened sky, illuminated by stars shining like stories waiting beneath the surface. They knew that with each shared account, the legacy of humanity continued to flourish, nurturing connections with echoing reminders of love and resilience, a strength that could bind people together across time and space, an endless circle of existence woven through the act of storytelling and remembrance.

Thank You, Wonderful Reader!

Wow! You made it to the end, and I couldn't be prouder of you. Thank you for joining me on this magical journey through the pages of this book! Your commitment to reading until the last sentence speaks volumes about your curiosity and adventurous spirit. I hope this ride was as exhilarating for you as it was for me while creating it. There's nothing like the connection forged through shared words and ideas.

As you close this book, I encourage you to take a moment to reflect on what you've discovered. What insights grabbed your attention? Which characters stayed with you long after the book was shut? I genuinely hope that you found nuggets of wisdom that resonate and will spark conversations in your life. Transformative journeys often begin with a single thought, and I believe this book can be just that catalyst for you.

You've traveled through various landscapes of imagination and experience, and now, armed with fresh perspectives, you're ready to take on the world. Don't just leave this adventure behind; carry it with you! Share your thoughts, challenge the ideas presented, and let those sparks ignite new conversations with family, friends, or even strangers.

Your voice has power, and it's time to unleash it!

Remember, this isn't just an ending; it's a beginning. The stories and insights within these pages can influence actions, decisions, and ultimately, the course of your life. I hope you are inspired to implement some newfound knowledge, question your assumptions, or even dive deeper into the subjects we've explored together. You're now part of a broader conversation, and what you do with it is up to you!

As we part ways, know that my gratitude for your engagement is overflowing. Thank you for making this journey together, for letting the words resonate, and for being open to the unexpected twists and turns of this narrative. I'm excited for what you will take from this experience and can't wait for the adventures that await you. Let's keep pushing boundaries and exploring new horizons together, even if it's apart. So, here's to the future and all the stories yet to be written! Until we meet again, keep that spark alive and continue your quest for knowledge, connection, and growth. The world is your oyster, and I believe you're ready to shine! With all my deepest gratitude and warm wishes, With a heart full of appreciation